DEPRESSION KIDS

Revised Edition

JAMES EDWIN ALEXANDER

Macedon Publishing Co. : Oklahoma City

METROPOLITAN LIBRARY SYSTEM
"SERVING OKLAHOMA COUNTY"

Alexander, James Edwin, 1930--

ISBN 939965-19-4

The paper in this book meets the guidelins for permanence and durability of the Committee on Production Guidelines for Book Longevity of the Council on Library Resources, Inc.

Copyright © 1992, 2000 by Macedon Publishing Co., Oklahoma City. All rights reserved. Manufactured in the U.S.A.

1 2 3 4 5 6 7 8 9 10

Contents

	Preface	v
1.	High Expectations	1
2.	Bitterness and Pride	14
3.	Depression Blues	27
4.	Dust Bowl Years	42
5.	Hard Times	52
6.	The Hungry Years	61
7.	Illusions of Normalcy	77
8.	Bare Feet and Bib Overalls	98
9.	Rejection and Abandonment	118
10.	Almost Makin' It	137
11.	Pastures of Plenty	160
12.	Movin' On	166
13.	The End of the Beginning	183
14.	Epilogue	195

DEDICATED TO

My brothers and sisters

PREFACE

In the minds of many people who actually lived it, the struggle that was the Great Depression was neither great nor noble. They see a time pitted by deep caverns of suffering, humans reduced to the lowest level of existence. They remember people bowed to indignities and suffused with shame for reasons they knew not.

Certainly as I have lived these stories and talked about them with members of my family, I have been struck by the sheer brutality of it all. Many of the details are so gruesome I didn't feel comfortable about writing them here.

The Great Depression and Dust Bowl occurred 60 to 70 years ago. Why have we remembered that era so long? Why so well?

Because these patterns were indelibly etched into our daily lives. There are many details we would just as soon forget. Yet they live in us with a depth of feeling that will not go away.

To me, the Depression Era provides a proud statement of man's strength, a parable of human endurance and transcendence at a time it seemed impossible. I see people not on their knees but on their feet, seeking to hang on to their pride and dignity. I see my mother's determination, doggedly positive in an era of great negativity. I see my father, born of promise and dashed to degradation.

And now, sixty years after the fact, I fully understand just how intimately the Depression Era was involved in shaping the character of our lives. The whole story looms before me as a metaphor, a thread so intricately woven into the fabric of time that its pattern reflects the heart and soul of the people who lived it.

The pieces of this puzzle--my pattern, you might say--have fallen into place for me now. To begin, I collected as many pieces of history as I could; I searched my memory for recollections of events from my personal experience; I tried to remember tales my parents had told--but who, alas, are no longer here to verify them; I tried to put myself in their shoes and see things from their point of view. I have talked with my brothers and sisters about their individual experiences and perspectives. And through it all, I have reached certain conclusions that are born as much from feeling as they are from fact.

The closer I look into those times, the more important they are to me. The people, who with their heart and strength made life mean something, were tough, gentle folk who bore their burden with a stamina that seems remarkable today. Some had barely enough grit to see it through, but all had some measure of strength, purpose, and will to live and transcend, a desire to build--and when that failed--to rebuild again and again.

In today's "too comfortable" society, the kind of blood, sweat and tears displayed by our parents seems without compare. Today's problems seem tame when measured against those of our parents' day. But hopefully, the victories they won and the lessons we learned can help us meet the challenges of our time. If ever we should find ourselves in the midst of such a severe test, perhaps their victories and lessons will provide us the strength and endurance to tough it through.

The will to survive represents the real treasure born of the Depression years, a bright spot of color that shone through those darkest of days. It underlies the human values of courage, hope, generosity, determination and love that can never be lost so long as our families live--and remember.

Grateful acknowledgement is given to my sisters Catherine and Shirley who assisted mightily in gathering material for this book, and to Katherine Yates for editorial services. Finally, the views expressed are those of the author alone and do not necessarily reflect those of other family members.

--James Edwin Alexander
October, 2000

Adapted from: Gene Florence, The Collector's Encyclopedia of Depression Glass, 9th ed., Collectors Books, 1990

1

High Expectations

The Firstborn
The Great Depression and I were born almost at the same time. The stock market collapsed October 24, 1929. I came along four months later, February 16, 1930. Hence, my childhood years paralleled the longest and most severe depression ever experienced by the Western industrialized world.

"Black Thursday," as October 24 became known, created panic in the financial markets. President Herbert Hoover sought to reassure the American people. "I am of the opinion that this reaction has badly overrun itself," he said.

Meanwhile, far away from Wall Street, on the fertile farmland of Iowa where my parents and grandparents lived, tilled the soil, and raised their families, there was little awareness of the troubles and travails facing New York's money moguls. Crops abounded, land was appreciating in value, and farmers faced the future with high expectations.

My mother, the former Lillian Gamble, was seventeen, just two weeks shy of her eighteenth birthday. For four days she had lain writhing and bathed in sweat in the front bedroom of her mother's Iowa farmhouse, often delirious, stricken with bronchial pneumonia. On Saturday, February 15, young Dr. Trueblood was called. He drove out from town. There was no treatment he could offer. Pneumonia was a disease for which there was no known cure, a dreaded killer of children and old folks.

Dr. David Trueblood was a tall slender man of thirty. He had brown, wavy hair and slightly stooped shoulders. He exuded an air of quiet confidence. Less than five years out of medical school at the University of Iowa, he seemed wise beyond his years. Already the citizenry had bestowed upon him the sobriquet "Doc," a title of honor they usually reserved for beloved elder physicians.

The doctor advised Lillian's mother to feed her daughter aspirin, bathe her with cold compresses to keep down the fever, and rub generous amounts of Vicks VapoRub on her chest. The disease would have to run its course. Apart from that, he said, all they could do was hope and pray her fever would soon break. The next twenty-four hours should tell the tale. "It's in the Lord's hands now," he told her.

Adding to the worry, Lillian was eight-and-a-half months pregnant with her first child. Not only was the mother's life at stake but also the life of her unborn baby. Trueblood advised if Lillian went into convulsions, they should call him immediately. He would try to save the child's life, even if he were unable save the mother. There was a chance the baby could be brain damaged by the mother's sustained high fever.

Lillian was Ed and Mae Gamble's fifth child and second daughter. Three boys had been born first, Raymond, Walter and Eddie, then a daughter, Mildred. My mother came along four years later. Then came two more daughters, Ruth and Catherine. Another son, Charles, brought the total to eight. Mildred, closest to my mother in age, was an "indoor" girl who clung to her mother; whereas my mother was a tomboy. She worked outdoors alongside her dad and brothers doing farm chores and helping build a new addition to the barn.

Normally fun-loving and infectiously friendly, Lillian now appeared strangely weak and fragile lying on her mother's bed. She was tall and large-boned, five feet eight and 135 pounds. She wore her soft, brunette hair cut in a boyish bob. Laughter danced in her eyes. Although not labeled a "pretty" girl, she had a sensuous beauty that made her attractive to members of the opposite sex.

My dad, Eugene Alexander, better known as "Gene," was not present for the birth. He was in South Dakota.
Only nineteen, he was trying to start a new farm in South Dakota. The previous summer, his parents, Jesse and Addie Alexander, swapped their 160-acre Iowa farm for a three-quarters section of land near Artesian, South Dakota. They persuaded Gene, the baby of the family, that he ought to move up there to be near them. With his father's help, my dad rented some land about a mile away. My mother stayed behind to have her baby. She planned to join him as soon as the child was old enough to travel.

My parents probably should never have gotten married. It was a case of "have to."
Eugene Alexander was active in 4-H. He'd won nearly every prize at the county and state levels. Only one trophy remained, and that was to win the *Chicago International*. This was the "World Series" of 4-H. In 1929, Eugene took his prize steer to the *International*. He won Grand Champion. He was, so to speak, on top of the world.
When he came back home he took his girlfriend, Lillian Gamble, out to celebrate. Perhaps they celebrated a little too much. Lillian got pregnant.
They didn't tell anybody; they quietly drove across the border to Missouri for a "quickie" marriage. Now, seven months later, Lillian was about to deliver.

As Dr. Trueblood left the farm house that Saturday afternoon, the weather outside turned nasty. What began earlier in the day as a light, misty rain now turned to sleet. The temperature plunged, and soon the ground was covered with a solid sheet of ice. The wind picked up.
"Taint a fit day out for man or beast," Ed Gamble grumbled as he struggled to pull on his heavy sheepskin coat and five-buckle

overshoes. It was time to bring in the cows for their evening feeding and milking.

The Gamble farm lay two-and-a-half miles southwest of Indianola, Iowa. To get there, one took a two-lane gravel highway west from town. A turn south on a dirt road at Two-Mile Corner took one past Hoosier Row School and over a rickety one-lane log bridge that spanned South River. The two-story Gamble house had been built out of native timber by Lillian's grandfather, LeRoy Gamble, Civil War veteran and one of the original settlers in this area.

Shortly after midnight, Lillian passed through her "crisis." The fever broke dramatically. She fell into a deep sleep of exhaustion. Mae Gamble sat throughout the night in the chair beside her daughter's bed.

Sunday morning dawned cold and clear. Only a few wispy mare's tail clouds gently brushed the sky overhead. Outside, it was a fairyland of ice. Glistening crystals coated naked trees, telephone lines, and fence-rows, illuminated by golden rays of the morning sun.

It was nearly ten when Lillian awoke from her healing sleep. "Mom," she cried weakly.

Mae, who was in the kitchen preparing Sunday dinner, rushed to her daughter's bedside. "Are you all right?" she asked apprehensively.

"Mom, I'm starting to feel cramps in my tummy," Lillian complained.

Mae placed her hand on Lillian's bulging stomach. She could feel movement. The baby was ready to come into the world. "You're having labor pains," she said. "I'm going to get Doc Trueblood."

The hand-crank telephone was mounted on a wall inside the front door. Mae lifted the receiver off the hook and held it to her ear to make sure no one else was talking on the rural line. She gave the handle three hard cranks and waited for the operator to answer. "Get me Doctor Trueblood."

She waited.

"There's no answer," the operator said.

"Did you try both his office and his home?" Mae asked.

"Yes."

"Then try the Quaker Church. He may have left for Sunday School."

"The Quaker Church doesn't have a telephone."

"Then call one of the neighbors and have them go over to the church," Mae said impatiently. "Tell him to come out to the Gamble farm right away. It's an emergency." With that, she hung up.

Less than ten minutes later, the telephone rang. Two longs and a short. That was the Gamble ring. Dr. Trueblood came on the line.

"Doctor, can you come out?" Mae asked anxiously. "I think Lillian's going into labor."

"How's her fever?"

"It's gone. It broke about midnight."

"That's good." He paused. "How are the roads out your way?"

"Everything's covered with ice. Ed says you'll be okay on the main highway. He doesn't think a car can make it down our road, though. He'll have one of the boys hitch up a team and wagon and meet you at Two Mile Corner to bring you the rest of the way."

At 12:10 p.m., Lillian delivered a son. He weighed six pounds, ten ounces. As nearly as the doctor could tell, the child was normal.

"What name are you going to give him?" Dr. Trueblood asked as he filled out the certificate of birth.

"James Edwin," Lillian announced proudly, tickling her child fondly on the cheeks to see him smile. "*James* is for his father, and *Edwin* is for my father." Trueblood looked quizzical. She explained that Eugene's given name was James.

Initially they had planned on naming me "Jesse," after Eugene's father. However, just three weeks earlier that name had been preempted by a son born to Eugene's older brother, Merlin.

My mother's troubles were not over. I failed to thrive. Dr. Trueblood was called back to the Gamble farm two weeks later. They told him I was colicky, unable to keep nourishment down, and running freely at the other end. My weight dropped to barely six pounds.

Trueblood determined there was something wrong with Lillian's milk that inadvertently was causing her to "poison" her own baby--possibly triggered by her bout with pneumonia. He suggested she take me off the breast and put me on cow's milk laced with a teaspoon of white Karo syrup. Apparently it worked, for I immediately began to show improvement.

I was six weeks old when Grandpa Gamble drove Mom and me twenty-two miles into Des Moines. There he put us on a train that would take us to South Dakota.

Lillian was apprehensive about saying good-bye to her father. Ed Gamble, only 53, was diagnosed as having multiple sclerosis. In all probability, that meant he wouldn't have many years to live. She feared she might never see her father alive again.

They say I rode alongside Mom in a wicker basket, cushioned by an embroidered pillow Grandma Gamble made for me. The rumbling of the train made a soothing sound. Mom says I slept most of the journey in my favorite position--face down, rump stuck up in the air, and sucking the first two fingers of my right hand.

Dad met the train the following day at Mitchell, South Dakota. From Mitchell, it was a 30-mile drive to the Alexander farm.

South Dakota Farm - 1930

Eugene's farm comprised 240 acres of windswept-prairie five miles north of the town of Artesian. On it sat a weathered wood-frame, two-story house, a dilapidated red barn with haymow, machinery shed, granary and, of course, a two-seater outhouse.

Artesian was a struggling farming community on the plains of east-central South Dakota, located some thirty miles north of Mitchell--home of the Corn Palace. It was nineteen miles east of Woonsocket, the county seat of Sanborn County. The 1930 Census reported the town's population at 556 people, 133 less than the 1920 Census.

Founded in 1883, Artesian took its name from the artesian wells in the area. An underground stream flowed beneath the surface of the ground, trapped under great pressure between two layers of rock. When a well was drilled into the stream through the overlying layer of rock, pressure forced the water to rise to the surface. In some cases, water shot as much as 130 feet into the air.

The artesian well in the front yard of our house spouted water as hard as nails and cold enough to crack your teeth.

The house, the barn, and main part of the farm were situated on the west side of the road. The granary and machinery shed were directly across to the east on an adjoining eighty acres. At one time, this east eighty had been a separate farm. Its owners had long since pulled up stakes and moved out. Only a foundation remained as a visible reminder of where the house had once stood, plus a couple of outbuildings and some rusting machinery.

There were four rooms on the ground floor of the Alexander home--a kitchen, dining room, front room, and bedroom. The dining and front rooms were separated by folding doors which could be opened out to make one big room when we had company. Upstairs, four sleeping rooms were arranged more or less on a similar layout as the downstairs rooms. They were not nearly as spacious because the roof slanted inward at a low angle. The sloping ceilings cut off part of the usable space and made the rooms seem more like lofts. A single, narrow flight of steep stairs led upward from the living room. The bottom was closed off by a door to avoid wasting precious heat in the wintertime.

On the east, or front side of the house, a tiny covered porch looked out on the road. Leading off the kitchen on the back side of the house was a utility porch with a wash stand and water bucket. There the menfolk could wash off caked layers of sweat and dust from the fields before coming into the house. A grove of trees stood between the house and the road.

Our neighbor to the south was George Callahan--"Crazy George," as the farmers thereabouts were wont to call him. He had a peculiar habit of sipping only hot water instead of drinking coffee or stronger stuff. Unmarried, George lived with his mother until her death. He probably never would marry.

On the next farm to the north lived the Keelers. They had two teen-age boys and an "old-maid" daughter who still lived at home. Farmers around there considered it a curse to have a daughter over the age of 25 who couldn't find a husband, and they made no bones about referring to her as an "old maid."

Of all the young men who ever had visions of farming, few were better qualified or showed more promise than Eugene Alexander. Though not a large man--standing only about five-nine and weighing in at 145 pounds--he had acquired a reputation for hard work and ability that far exceeded his size. In the farming community west of Indianola where he grew up, one often heard the comment, "Boy, there's no one who can shock grain like Gene Alexander," or, "Man, that Gene Alexander sure knows how to stack hay."

He was the youngest of five children, and his mother's pet. She let his hair grow in long ringlets and never cut it until the day he started school. Success came early and easily for him, but he had never ben tested in the cruel crucible of adversity.

At age nineteen, Eugene Alexander felt ready to take on the world.

Eugene learned that the soil here on the windy plains of central South Dakota was not as fertile as that where he grew up in Iowa. That meant he would have to work harder to scratch out a living. Down around Indianola, the rich, black loam ran eight to ten inches deep and would grow most any kind of crop. Here, there was just barely enough topsoil to cover the sandy clay underneath. What soil there was had a tendency to blow around in the wind if left unprotected. Iowa corn grew fourteen feet tall and yielded a hundred bushels to the acre; here the scrawny stalks yielded barely half as much. And whereas Iowa farmers grew good cover crops of oats, barley, and alfalfa, the South Dakota farmers tended to plant their acreage in wheat, year after year after year.

Had Eugene gone into wheat farming, he would have enjoyed certain advantages. Wheat is a low-maintenance crop. Planted early in the spring, it grows without further supervision. A single farmer could plant hundreds of acres, and--provided it's not damaged by drought or plague--sit back and watch it grow. Harvest time--generally mid to late August--brought a second round of intense activity. But once the crop was hauled off to the elevator and sold to market, the wheat farmer was through for the year. His time was pretty much his own until the next spring's planting.

The downside of wheat farming was the way it was practiced. By not rotating the crops, the already poor condition of the soil was depleted a little bit more each year. And what the land no longer yielded in bushels per acre, the farmer made up by planting more acres.

Another problem was that the harvested wheat field did not offer good soil cover. The ground lay bare to the ravages of the wind for eight months of the year. Already, several large dust storms had blown through the area.

Eugene Alexander, however, was imbued with the cockiness that only a nineteen-year-old can have. He would show these South Dakota farmers a thing or two. He was going to be a "stock" farmer. That was what he knew best; it was where he found his early success.

Instead of raising grain for the market, the stock farmer planted crops that were intended primarily for consumption by his own livestock. When fattened for market, prime beef would fetch a healthy price at the stockyards. Eugene calculated that there was more profit to be made in feeding cattle than in raising wheat.

The problem with stock farming is that it is labor intensive. Cattle have to be fed morning and evening, summer and winter, and Sundays without fail. They must be dehorned and vaccinated, dewormed and detoxified. To keep them in feed, Eugene planted the fields with corn, oats, barley and hay. The cornfields had to be cultivated to rid it of weeds until the stalks were waist-high in mid July. Then it was time for the first hay cutting, which had to be hauled into barns or stacked in the field. Next, it was time to harvest the oats and barley. Following that, the second cutting of hay. When October came around, it was time to husk corn. The winter months were spent hauling manure out of the barn and repairing machinery. And always, the livestock needed to be tended.

Life on the farm was never easy. Eugene's work day began every morning before 6:00 o'clock doing chores. At 8:00, he came in for breakfast--a half-dozen eggs, a slab of side meat, and a mess of greasy fried potatoes washed down with cups of scalding coffee. Then it was out to the fields.

At ten, Lillian would carry a "lunch" out to him, normally a sandwich and a tin pail of steaming coffee. Dinner, at noon, was the main meal of the day. Eugene could stow away prodigious amounts of food. After fifteen minutes or so of snoozing while his food settled, it was back to the fields.

After a late afternoon lunch at 3:30, he worked until six when he came in to do the evening chores. Supper was usually at eight or eight-thirty--earlier in winter months and later in summer. After supper, Eugene generally dozed while sitting upright in his rocking chair. At nine-thirty or so, he would light a kerosene lantern and go out to check the animals. Then to bed.

Grandpa's Farm

Grandpa Alexander's farm was just a mile west of our house--as the crow flies, but double that on the road. Both farm houses were situated in the middle of their respective sections, so to get from Dad's place to Grandpa's, one had to drive a half mile south, a mile west, then a half mile north again.

Grandpa's house stood on the west side of the road, facing east.

Like Dad's, it was two-storied with a small porch on the front and a utility porch on the back. The only really noticeable difference was that Grandpa's driveway curved away from the house toward the south, whereas Dad's driveway curved around toward the north.

At age fifty-eight, Jesse Alexander looked a little like Hollywood's version of a judge. He was above average height with brownish hair graying at the temples and a bald spot showing at the crown of his head. He wore a somber expression that was belied by the laughter wrinkles radiating outward from his eyes. He was never in a hurry, seldom moved to anger, and methodically got things done.

Family lore has it that one of the few times Jesse Alexander was roused to unexpected action occurred when I was six months old, and teething. Mom and Dad had gone over to Grandpa's for Sunday dinner. They sat around in the living room talking after the meal. Mom was bouncing me on her lap, when I bit her on the arm. She fussed at me, and I began to cry.

Grandpa scolded Mom, "Don't fuss at James that way. He's just a little baby. He doesn't know he's doing anything wrong. Here, let me take him. I'll show you how to hold a baby." (He'd had experience with five of his own, plus eight grandchildren.)

He took me into his arms, held me up against his shoulder, patted me on the back, and rocked gently back and forth. "There, there," he said soothingly. "Grandpa hold James. Grandpa show mommy how to hold little James."

About the time he got me settled comfortably and picked up the thread of conversation, I sank my teeth into Grandpa's neck. Real hard. Grandpa let out a screech and came out of his chair. "Here, you take him!" he ordered Lillian, holding me out at arms length. Mom said it was all she could do to keep from laughing.

Grandma was as different from Grandpa as two married people could be. She was high-strung, headstrong, and a perfectionist. Whatever she set her mind to do, she "would" do. She was always getting on Jesse to do this, or take care of that.

"Now Addie...." he would say condescendingly, trying to calm her down. When the air got too heated, he'd simply go outside, hitch up the wagon and go for a ride. I saw a lot of countryside riding beside my Grandpa that way. Jesse's habit that annoyed his wife the most was he chewed tobacco and had to have a spittoon beside his chair. Some people suggested that the only reason he continued to chew tobacco was to annoy Addie.

My Grandma, the former Addie Gertrude Yant, was born in Altoona, Iowa, in 1878. She married Jesse Alexander at age nineteen. He was six years older.

The Yants were among the early settlers in Polk County, Iowa. The town of Altoona had originally been named Yant until the Rock Island Railroad came through in 1867 and changed the name. Her father and brothers were not pleased that she married Jesse Alexander. The Yants were breeders of fine horses, and they looked disdainfully upon ordinary dirt farmers like the Alexanders. Besides, the Yant men all stood well over six feet tall, while Jesse Alexander hardly came up to their shoulders. In truth, Addie's family never expected Jesse to amount to much.

Addie was a tall, slender woman. Her once willowy figure was only now, at age fifty-two, beginning to show signs of thickening about the waist. She continued to fashion her reddish-brown, now graying, hair in set waves that had been the style of her girlhood.

Addie excelled at whatever she set her mind to do. She never accepted anything less than her very best. She was the champion cake baker at the Iowa State Fair for twenty-three out of twenty-five years. In all, she won 156 first place awards for various home crafts. In 1923, she entered the national Pillsbury Bake-Off contest and took first place. The following year, her picture and personal endorsement were used in newspaper and magazine ads for Knox Gelatin, Swans Down Cake Flour, and the Perfection Stove Company.

One of my earliest memories is riding on Grandpa's McCormack-Deering 10-30 tractor. It was a huge monster of a machine, weighing over five thousand pounds and rolling on steel, lugged wheels that were taller than a man's head. The machine moved ponderously slow, not capable of more than six miles an hour in high gear. Sometimes Grandpa let me ride on his lap while he worked the fields, letting me believe I was actually steering the contraption. Later, Grandpa bragged to Grandma how hard I worked that morning. Grandma, for her part, showered me with praise and fixed a special treat.

There also came a time when Grandma was not amused with me. That happened one Thanksgiving when Dad's sister, Florence, and her husband, Raymond, came up from Iowa with their two children, Dale and Faune. Dale was five years older than me, Faune two.

Grandma set a big Thanksgiving table, of which she was justly proud. She invited the new minister and his wife and the Jenske's from down the road to share in the repast. All in all, there were ten grown-ups and five kids around the table.

After the meal was over but before the dishes had been cleared, I noticed two plump, uneaten sausages still laying on the serving platter. "Grandma," I asked, "Who poo-pooed on the plate?"

Grandma was so mortified she ordered Dad to take me out of her house. Moreover, she said, I was not to return until I learned some proper manners.

Oh, the mule's gone lame and the hens won't lay,
Corn's way down, wheat don't pay,
Hogs no better, steer's too cheap,
Cows quit milking and the meat won't keep.
Oats all heated, spuds all froze,
Wheat crop's busted, wind still blows,
Looks some gloomy, I'll admit,
But git up, dobbin, we ain't down yet.
--Tune: "Turkey in the Straw"
--Words: *Farmers' Union Bulletin*

2

Bitterness and Pride

Catherine's Birth

In the spring of 1931, when I was barely one, major changes began taking place inside the body of my mother. Of course, I couldn't have known it at the time, but a new baby was growing in her tummy. The baby was due the end of May.

Lillian planned to ride the train to Indianola to have the new baby at her mother's home. She "hated" living in South Dakota and didn't want her child born there. Too, she was worried about reports concerning her father's deteriorating health. He was going downhill rapidly. These were trying times for her.

On Saturday, April 18th, just a week before she was scheduled to leave for Iowa, Lillian was still performing her farm-wife's duties. She fixed an afternoon lunch of sandwiches and a pail of coffee for Dad and the hired hand, and then headed out to the field to deliver it to them. She was wearing a red dress that day.

Unthinkingly, she took a shortcut across the cow pasture. Eugene's mean-spirited bull charged toward her. Frightened for her life, Lillian made a mad race towards the fence. She got there just ahead of the bull. However, when she attempted to jump over the fence to safety, she caught her foot on the top strand and fell heavily.

That night she delivered a baby girl. Eugene sent the hired man into town to get Dr. F. W. Loring when she went into labor. For the past forty-six years, Loring, nearing seventy, had been the town's doctor. He came right away.

The baby was born shortly after midnight. She was six weeks premature and weighed only four pounds two ounces. She came out with the umbilical cord wrapped around her neck. Her skin color was blue. The baby lacked sufficient oxygen. Her breathing was shallow and rapid. Dr. Loring feared the child might have a heart defect.

Rubbing and patting her chest didn't work. Dr. Loring, in desperation, tried breathing into the child's mouth to fill her tiny lungs with rich, moist air. That seemed to bring some improvement. He put her in a shoe box and placed it on the opened oven door of the kitchen stove to keep her body warm. Throughout the night he and Dad took turns breathing into her.

Lillian named the baby "Catherine Aline," combining the first name of her sister Catherine with the middle name of her sister Ruth.

Grandma Alexander got upset when she and Grandpa came over for a visit the next day and learned that little Catherine had already been born. Why wasn't she called? The truth was, Lillian didn't want her there. Addie was too domineering and rigid. Understandably, she felt slighted.

Addie became doubly upset when she learned that Lillian had named the baby after two sisters. Addie thought they had an understanding the first son would be named after the two grandfathers--hence James Edwin. And in like manner, Lillian would name her first daughter after the two grandmothers, which would have been "Addie Mae."

Conventional medical wisdom called for a new mother to spend ten days in bed following childbirth. Since Lillian was unable to make the journey to Indianola herself, she asked her mother to come up to South Dakota to take care of her during the lying-in period.

The two grandmothers sniped and fussed at each other as how best to care for the baby. Addie Alexander came from the school of thought that said a baby should be propped up on its back with a pillow at each side so it couldn't turn its head. As a result, all five of her kids were flat-headed in back. Every chance she got, she turned Catherine on her back and propped pillows alongside her head.

Mae Gamble, on the other hand, believed a baby should be cuddled. She spent hours with Catherine lying face down on her lap, rubbing and patting her.

The local diet didn't set well with Mae Gamble. Each morning Eugene went out and shot a couple of pheasants. Mae hated to clean those damn birds. Worse, a diet rich with pheasant meat and artesian well water gave her a bad case of green-apple trots.

Lillian was able to watch out her bedroom window as Mae trotted to the outhouse where she would do her duty, start back toward the house, then turn around again and head back to the outhouse. Lillian thought that was funny and teased her mother about it. Mae got real grumpy and retorted, "I don't think that's funny at all. I've worn out a pair of new shoes since I've been here."

Catherine was born when I was only fourteen months old. Mom just turned nineteen, was married less than two years, and already she had two kids in diapers.

I'm sure that initially I saw the new baby as exciting, something new in the family, like having a new toy. I liked to hug the baby, touch her and kiss her--particularly when there was an audience. People would say, "See how James loves his little sister."

My attitude began to change after the first few weeks, however.

The novelty wore off. Gradually, I came to the realization that this new addition was here to stay. I was having to give up my place in the family. I was going to have to share my parents' affection with this intruder. At that point I began to poke and pinch the baby and do things that expressed my feelings of rejection.

But after another few weeks, my feelings leveled off and I began to enjoy my little sister. Indeed, I became exceedingly protective of her.

House Fire

On January 29, 1932, two weeks before my second birthday, our house caught on fire. The temperature was near zero. Patchy snow covered the ground. Leaden clouds scudded across the sky. Mom had gone out to the chicken coop to tend a new brood of baby chicks. Catherine, nine months old, was in a jump swing suspended from the doorway between the living and dining rooms. I was playing in the kitchen. It was four o'clock in the afternoon.

Mom came around the corner of the chicken coop and turned toward the house. Flames were curling up around the kitchen and back porch. She ran towards the house, screaming for her husband, "Eugene, Eugene, Eugene."

"Oh my God, my babies are in there," she cried as she pulled frantically on the kitchen door. The flames blew out at her. They singed off her eyebrows and the front of her hair.

Dad heard her screams and ran from the barn.

"James and Catherine are still in there!" Mom yelled at him.

"Where are they?" he demanded. "Where did you leave them?"

"Catherine is in her swing. James was in the kitchen."

Flames raged the highest in the kitchen. That's probably where the fire started. Entry through that part of the house was impossible. Dad's best hope was to go around to the back side of the house and break a window far away from the flames. That way, he sought to avoid creating a draft that would make the flames worse.

Once he gained entrance, Dad crawled along the floor under the smoke looking for his two children. He found Catherine right where Mom said she would be, in her jump swing. I was beside the swing trying to protect my little sister. Apparently, I was trying to lift her out of the swing, but she was too heavy for me. Nonetheless, I was trying to do something.

Dad wrapped Catherine in his coat and, choking on smoke, crawled back through the living room and bedroom to the broken window. He handed her out to her distraught mother.

"Where's James? Where's James?" Mom begged of him.

"He's in there. I'm going back to get him."

Dad filled his lungs with deep draughts of fresh, clean air before he crawled back to rescue his firstborn. He found me still sitting where he had told me to wait.

The house was a complete loss. By the time neighbors got there to help, the structure was too far gone to save. Besides, there was no fire-fighting equipment. They managed to salvage only a few possessions from the bedroom and living room. One of the items saved was Dad's prized chest of ribbons and trophies he had won in 4-H.

We spent the night at Grandpa's house. The next day, Saturday, some neighbors had come over. They were sitting in the dining room, drinking coffee, and talking about the fire.

I lolled around in Grandma's green wingback chair in the parlor that sat just inside the front door. A faint, musty smell emanated from the faded upholstery. I was alone in the parlor. The grown-ups were in the next room.

I could hear the grown-ups talking. It was extremely frustrating to me. My most indelible memory is of not being able to remember. I knew what they were talking about, but I couldn't remember the fire itself. No matter how hard I tried, I couldn't conjure up any pictures in my head. I didn't understand why I couldn't remember.

Later that afternoon, everybody drove over to look at the remains of what had been our home. Hardly a timber stood above ground. Mom cried. But for me it was an adventure. Rummaging through the ashes I found a pocketknife that Grandpa had given me for Christmas; the blade would still open but the green side panels had been burned off with just the rivets sticking out.

An old, weathered granary sat across the road east of our now-destroyed house. Neighbors pitched in and helped Dad convert it into temporary living quarters. It measured twenty-four feet by twenty-four feet and had no interior walls. It was not built with the idea human beings would someday be living in it.

They tacked up tar paper on the inside to keep the wintry wind from blowing between the cracks. A partition ran across from east to west to divide the space into two parts. The south side was used as the kitchen-dining-living room. The north side became the sleeping quarters. Mom rigged some burlap to drape off a smaller section for Catherine and me to sleep.

That summer, we had another fire. It happened while Mom was getting ready to bake the weekly supply of bread.

Mom cooked on a Perfection brand kerosene stove that Grandma loaned her. The Perfection stove was a modern invention, clean and efficient. It could also be temperamental. The stove burned gasified kerosene fuel on burners much like those found on more conventional gas ranges. There was a little tank of kerosene on the front with a plunger-type hand pump. It was necessary to pump up the pressure in the tank, then turn on the burners and light them with a match. When everything worked right, the stove produced a hot, stable, and smokeless flame.

The stove sat right inside the front door--in fact, the "only" door in or out of the makeshift dwelling. On this particular day, Mom finished filling the tank and pumped up the pressure. She apparently spilled a little raw kerosene, because when she lit the oven the whole thing blew up in her face. Flames shot up to the ceiling with a terrible WHOOSH.

Mom did not scream or panic. She coolly reached down and grabbed up Catherine and me and, taking one in each hand, she literally threw both of us out into the yard. Then she grabbed a nearly-full, hundred-pound sack of flour and threw it over the stove.

The flour smothered the fire. But it made a terrible mess of everything else. When Catherine and I ventured back inside to see what was going on, we saw our mother sitting in the middle of the floor, crying.

Big Brother

A bond developed between Catherine and me that was hard to explain. Perhaps it was because we were so close in age. We shared the same emotional and physical needs. We spent a lot of time together playing, exploring, and learning by ourselves. There weren't any other children around the farm most of the time. After Catherine was big enough to walk, we became as inseparable as twins.

I became Catherine's mentor. Often, I could be heard solemnly explaining to Catherine all about the stars and telescopes and science and things like that. Where I got that knowledge, I'll never know. Perhaps I made it up. Nevertheless, I said it with such great certitude that Catherine believed everything her big brother told her as being the absolute truth. If someone asked her a question which she couldn't answer, her stock reply was, "Ask James."

Catherine and I got lost one day. Or so the grownups thought. It happened one afternoon in August the summer that I was four and Catherine three.

Mom discovered us missing. In and of itself, that wasn't unusual. There were so many intriguing places to explore on a farm. She called for us to come in but got no answer. She checked all the usual places--the grove down by the road, the haymow, Dad's tool shed, upstairs in the house, and the farm pond. No kids anywhere.

By then, Mom was getting apprehensive. She thought maybe we had wandered out to the field where Dad and a crew of three were stacking bundles of grain into shocks. We weren't there either.

We had been missing for more than two hours. Dad called the hired hands to join the search. They scoured the pasture for fear we had been trampled by cows. They checked out the hog pen, knowing that dangerous old boar hogs have a bad reputation for attacking defenseless people. One searcher went down the road to check ditches along both sides in case we had been hit by a car. They dragged the pond. All to no avail.

Unaware of the hullabaloo we had created, Catherine and I emerged from the cornfield alongside the fence-row, walking hand in hand. I had taken my little sister for a walk and was serenely explaining how living things grow.

"We weren't lost, Mom," I said, puzzled by my parents' agitation. "I knew where we were all the time."

Catherine went through a phase of being quite a tattle-tale. She would run up, "Mom, Mom, James did this...." or, "Mom, Mom, do you know what James just did?" Mom didn't like it one bit and tried to break her of the habit.

One afternoon, Catherine and I played out by the chicken coop. One of the Rhode Island Reds had just hatched a brood of a dozen chicks. All of the baby chicks were fuzzy yellow except for one which was a mottled brown. I thought the brown chick was one of the prettiest things I had ever seen, so I tried to catch it to play with. The chick darted away. In the process of chasing it I stepped on the poor thing. The chick died a gruesome death, its entrails trailing out on the ground.

Catherine ran into the house as fast as her chubby legs would carry her. "Mom, Mom," she called out. "James stepped on a baby chicken and its guts are all squished out."

Instead of my being punished, however, Catherine got a rude surprise. Mom paddled her for tattling.

One Wednesday afternoon, Catherine and I played in the ditch alongside the road. I reached into the pocket of my overalls and pulled out a book of paper matches that I had found in the house. I was going to teach Catherine how to light a fire.

The wind was blowing so strongly that the matches went out immediately when I struck them. I couldn't get the fire to light. Finally, with only one or two matches left, I managed to get a small blaze going. The grass was too green to burn, however, and the fire petered out after having burned only a yard or so patch of area.

I promptly forgot all about it. Until the following Sunday, that is, when Mom and Dad had some friends over to the house. It was afternoon and they had finished eating. The menfolk sat around the kitchen with their chairs tilted back against the wall. They smoked hand-rolled cigarettes, sipped coffee, and told jokes. The women were in the living room. The kids were underfoot.

Mom said to me, "Go tell your father what you did."

I didn't know what she meant until she said, "You know, about lighting the fire...."

I thought I had done something wonderful. I assumed she wanted me to go in and tell Dad what a big boy I was. So I went into the kitchen, interrupted the men's conversation, and proudly related the story of lighting the fire.

Much to my chagrin, Dad was not amused. He came down hard off his chair, took me out on the front porch, and soundly paddled my bottom.

I felt betrayed. Not only did I suffer the pain of being spanked, there was also the humiliation of having it happen in front of all those people. I could hear the men laughing through the open window.

Dad's Pond

The Alexanders were one of the few families who had a private swimming pool. Actually, it was little more than an ordinary farm pond.

It came as a result of a government program to encourage farmers to build farm ponds as a means of slowing soil erosion.

Dad gratefully accepted his subsidy and used it to dig a pond about fifty yards south of the house. He was real proud of his creation. He felt he'd put one over on the government.

Dad dug it by himself using a road scraper he had acquired somewhere. The road scraper was a horse-drawn piece of machinery shaped something like an overgrown scoop shovel. It was three-and-a-half feet wide, had a drawbar to hitch a team to, and a pair of hardwood handles extending backwards two feet on each side. When filled to the brim, it carried five cubic feet of soil.

The scraper worked like this: Dad would hitch the team to the front of the scraper, position himself in back, and firmly grip the handles. He looped the reins around the back of his neck to control the horses. To fill the scraper, he would tilt its nose down into the soil. As soon as it scraped up a load of dirt, he would tilt it back to a slightly nose-up position and guide the horses to the dumping site. When he was ready to dump the dirt, he jerked the handles sharply upward which caused the scraper to flip over frontwards, spilling its payload.

Our pond was rectangular and measured fifty feet by fifty feet. It sloped downward to four feet at the deep end. The hard clay bottom did a good job of retaining water.

Dad also built an outdoor shower next to the pond. It was the only one of its kind in the vicinity. He sank two wooden beams in the ground which measured eight feet tall and spaced five feet apart. Between them, just above the height of a man's head, he mounted half of a fifty-gallon barrel that had been cut lengthwise. On the underneath side, he rigged a shower nozzle that could be turned on and off by pulling a chain.

The sun heated the water during the day. When Dad came in sweaty and dirty from the field he could have a nice, hot shower followed by a dip in the pool. Water for both the shower and the pond was amply supplied by an artesian well.

Catherine and I spent a lot of time in the pond during the long, hot South Dakota summer. I begged Mom for the loan of her copper boiler for use as a boat. Catherine and I took turns--first one, then the other--to get in it while the other pushed.

Young Driver

I took up driving at an early age. The afternoon of one July Fourth, Dad and Mom had company. The grownups sat in the house and visited. No one paid any attention to us kids. I decided to take Catherine for a drive.

Dad's Model-A Ford was parked on the grass out in front of the house. Catherine wasn't sure she liked the idea, but I solemnly assured her I knew how to drive. After all, I'd steered Grandpa's tractor, hadn't I? Also I'd seen how Dad made the car go by pushing a certain button on the floorboard. Over her misgivings, Catherine climbed into the car and wriggled up onto the front seat beside me.

I pushed the starter button and the car inched forward. But the engine didn't go. I was puzzled. I stepped on the button again, but the car didn't go very far this time either.

What I didn't know about a Model-A was that the starter motor would work without the ignition being turned on, but the engine wouldn't start until the key was turned. Undaunted, I kept mashing the starter button, and the car kept lurching forward, pulled solely by the power of its starter motor.

In the middle of the front yard was a twenty-foot flagpole that Dad had rigged out of galvanized steel pipe especially for this day. The car was aimed straight for that flagpole. But since I wasn't big enough to step on the starter button and steer the car at the same time, we ran right over the flagpole. Then the car stopped. It wouldn't go any farther.

When Dad came out of the house, he tried to figure out what happened. How in the world did the car get over there? Then he saw us kids. We were still in the car. "What are you doing?" he yelled.

Catherine began to cry. "James did it!"

At first, Dad was inclined to think it was funny--and he thanked his lucky stars nothing more serious had happened. But then he tried to move the car. It wouldn't budge. Its undercarriage was entangled on the metal pipe. That's when he got mad. Real mad. His speech turned the air blue.

I couldn't tell who Dad was maddest at, me or the car. I wasn't taking any chances, so I high-tailed it into the safety of the house as fast as my legs would carry me.

Dad had to get several men together to pick up the car and bodily lift it off the flagpole.

Barn Dance

Barn dancing made it easier to forget some of the worries of the Depression. These dances were great festive occasions in the farming community. Families came from miles around to attend.

The most popular ones were held on Saturday nights in mid-summer, between the time the farmer's haymow was emptied of last year's hay and before the new crop was hauled in. Occasionally one was held in the spring or fall.

The family hosting the event would sweep out their haymow to use as a dance floor and stack a few bales around the outer edge to serve as seats. A call was put out for fiddlers and guitar players. Anybody who brought along a musical instrument of any kind could usually get playing time.

Kids, as well as grownups, joined in the fun. There were tubs of sandwiches and cider. Some of the menfolk slipped out to a car during the evening to sneak a nip of stronger stuff.

Mom said that getting her husband to a dance was harder than pulling eye teeth. Dad complained that he was too tired after a full day's work to enjoy dancing.

Mom, on the other hand, was more of a free spirit and loved to dance. She accused Dad of marrying her under false pretenses. Before they were married they went dancing often, but since then he seldom went dancing at all.

A big dance was to be held over at the Tolbert's farm west of Artesian. Mom desperately wanted to go. But Dad, as usual, begged off, saying he was behind on getting the hay in. Mom persisted. Finally, Dad said he would do it on one condition, that she would agree to come out and work alongside him in the field to bring in the crop.

He tried to play a dirty trick on her. He thought if he worked Mom hard enough, she would get so tired she wouldn't want to go to the dance. But Mom was wise to his ways. She resolved that come hell or high water, he wasn't going to keep her from the dance. Tired to the point of exhaustion, she held him to his bargain. They went to that dance.

Little Catherine proved to be somewhat of an embarrassment at the dance. Somewhere, she had learned a grown-up joke and went around telling it to everybody even though she had little idea of what it meant. "Why don't trains have little trains and pencils have little pencils?" she asked anyone who would listen. Then she'd say, "Because pencils wear a rubber and trains pull out on time." But the more Mom tried to shush her up, the more Catherine felt compelled to blurt out her story.

If I could tell my troubles, it would
give my po' heart ease,
But depression has got me,
somebody help me please.
If I don't feel no better,
than I feel today,
I'm gonna pack my few clothes
and make my getaway.
--Song: "Depression Blues" - 1933

3

Depression Blues

Dick's Birth

By the fall of 1933, I three-and-a-half and old enough to begin being aware of my mother's physical appearance--specifically, what she looked like in comparison to other women. I was playing in the kitchen one morning while Mom cooked breakfast at the stove. She asked me to hand her something. When I looked up, I saw her in a new way. She was big and fat. I didn't know what to make of it. I couldn't remember her being that fat before.

What I didn't know was that she was pregnant. In just a few short weeks she would deliver her third child. I didn't comprehend the process of having babies.

Of course, I had seen farm animals born--puppies, kittens, lambs, and little pigs. I had watched Dad help deliver a calf. I had witnessed animals breeding, and I knew what that meant. Life was no mystery to me. However, I never translated this understanding of events from the animal world to the world of humankind. I hadn't connected my mother's bigness with her having a baby.

Mom, to me, was just Mom.

This time, Lillian made it to Indianola to have her child. She went by train, taking Catherine and me with her. We made the trip in the dead of winter.

During Lillian's absence, Eugene had to do his own cooking. He wasn't too keen on the idea, so he kept it simple. For every meal, he fixed himself fried potatoes, sausage and scrambled eggs--all cooked in the same skillet. He ate off the same dishes and silverware each time. He just kept throwing new grounds in the coffee pot without emptying the old. The pot soon filled up with rancid grounds.

The new baby was born December 19, 1933. I was almost four. Mom named him Richard Eugene--the "Eugene" being his dad's middle name. "Richard" was simply a name Mom liked. Since Dad wasn't present at the birth, he didn't have a say in the naming. From the start, though, everyone called the child "Dick."

Mom returned to South Dakota the middle of January. Traveling by train from Iowa with three tiny tots was a chore. She had to change trains twice, one of which was at night when Catherine and I were asleep. Other travelers were very helpful. One man carried me. Another carried the sleeping Catherine. Mom toted Dick in a wicker basket.

Dick was a long, skinny baby. He was also very sickly. He developed a milk allergy and couldn't keep anything down. He steadily lost weight.

Shortly after her return, Mom took Dick to see Grandpa Alexander, who was dying of cancer. She laid the sickly infant on the bed alongside the dying man. Grandpa looked down at Dick and said, "Well, little fella, we'll both be in the ground before the snow falls."

They tried several kinds of milk on Dick before finding one he could keep down. It was milk from one particular Guernsey cow owned by a neighbor. Every day for the next several months, someone went to the neighbor's house to get a half-gallon pail of milk.

As Dick's health improved, he became an animated baby, flailing his arms and legs a lot. He was a good-natured child who seldom fretted or cried. By the time he was six months old, he laughed and smiled at everyone, gurgling and cooing.

Mom placed Dick in the front yard one day when he was six months old for some sunshine and fresh air. She instructed me to keep an eye my little brother. It was a boring job.

I spied an old ladder leaning at a 45-degree angle against an elm tree in the front yard. I often enjoyed climbing that ladder. Seeing that ladder sparked an imaginative idea in my mind for entertaining my little brother.

I raided Dad's tool chest, got a hammer and nails, and commandeered Dick's blue blanket. I fashioned a kind of hammock between two rungs of the ladder, six feet off the ground. At the top edge I nailed the blanket to the ladder. The bottom edge of the blanket seemed long enough to drape over the lower rung and stay in place all by itself.

I picked up my baby brother and struggled to climb up the ladder with him. That proved to be a daunting task for a four-year-old. Nevertheless, I did it.

No sooner had I deposited Dick into the makeshift hammock than we both got a rude surprise. The unanchored bottom side of the blanket pulled free, Dick slid through the opening, and he fell kerplop on the ground.

Dick let out a squall. Mom rushed out of the house to see what was going on. Catherine excitedly reported the news: "Mom, Mom, James carried Dick up in the tree and dropped him on his head on the ground."

One afternoon when Dick was ten months old, Mom heard a muffled thump coming from the direction of the bedroom. Catherine ran out. "Mom, Mom, Dick fell out of his crib on his head."

Mom went to investigate. Dick was crawling across the floor hell bent for leather. "How did he get out of there?" Mom demanded, pointing towards the crib.

"He climbed out by himself," Catherine insisted.

"Don't lie to me, young lady!" Mom retorted. "There is no way that baby could have gotten out of that crib by himself."

Catherine continued to protest her innocence. Mom was faced with a mystery. No one else was in the room at the time. It was not plausible that a three-year-old Catherine could lift a twenty pound infant out of a crib that was taller than she. Mom put Dick back in his crib again.

A few minutes later, another thump. Here came Dick chugging along on all fours.

Once more, Mom put Dick back in his crib. This time she assigned me a chore. "James, you stay here and watch your little brother."

I watched as ordered. I was fascinated with what I saw.

Dick eyed his surroundings for a while. He pulled himself to a standing position inside the crib and maneuvered himself to where his head and arms were hanging over the side rail. He lunged with his body until his weight tilted him forward and over the edge of the crib. Down he went, landing headfirst on the floor. Dick got up onto his hands and knees crawled away lickety split, laughing like crazy.

Mom was convinced. She tried several ways to keep Dick in his crib. She looped rayon hose from one corner post to the other to raise the sides about six inches. Dick still managed to get himself out. She ordered a harness-type device from Montgomery Ward. Like a little Houdini, Dick wriggled himself out of that contraption too.

Three or four weeks after the crib episode, Catherine and I were upstairs cutting out pictures from the Montgomery Ward catalog. We heard a noise and looked around. Much to our amazement, here came Dick, crawling up the stairs to join us. He had never done that before.

Catherine was so surprised she let out a yell. That startled Dick. He reared up, lost his balance, and tumbled over backwards. He went end over end all the way to the bottom. But he didn't make so much as a whimper.

Mom was afraid he'd broken his neck or suffered some other

serious injury. But when she picked him up, all Dick did was laugh. He thought it was a game! No sooner did she put him back down on the floor than he made a beeline for the stairs to do it over again.

Dad fashioned a gate out of a screen door to keep Dick from getting to the stairs. Sometimes Catherine or I forgot and left the gate open. If someone didn't keep a constant eye on him, Dick would head for the stairs--often with the same result. It got to be a family joke. Whenever anyone heard a thump, thump, thump, they'd say, "There goes Dick again."

Despite his high activity level, Dick was late in learning to walk. At fourteen months, he still hadn't taken his first solo step. Perhaps because he was such an accomplished crawler, he didn't feel a need to walk.

One Sunday morning while Dad and Mom got ready to go into town, I amused my little brother by playing ball with him. Dick sat against one wall in the living room, spraddle-legged. I rolled the ball across the floor to him, and he trapped it between his outstretched legs. On one of those tosses, my aim wasn't too good. The ball bounced off Dick's foot and rolled to another part of the room out of his reach.

"Get ball. Get ball," Dick pleaded, reaching out toward the errant orb and wiggling his fingers frantically. I, however, growing bored with the game, ignored my brother's pleas.

A couple more entreaties went unheeded. Dick took matters into his own hands. He stood up and "ran" to where the ball was, picked it up and "ran" back to his former position.

I called for Mom and told her what happened. She didn't believe me. I took the ball and rolled it into a corner away from Dick. Sure enough, when I refused to retrieve the ball, Dick "ran" over and got it himself.

From then on, it was run, run, run. The child was in constant motion. He never walked any time he could run. Mom said it was a rare breed of person who learned to run before he learned to walk.

As Dick grew older, he became like a little Eugene. Wherever Dad went, Dick went too. If Dad went out to the barn with a pail to milk the cows, Dick trailed along with his own little pail to "milk" the little cows (calves). If Dad went to pee, Dick would pee, too.

Hard Winter

"It's cold enough out there to freeze the balls off a brass monkey," Eugene grumbled. He stamped his feet and rubbed his frostbitten cheeks. He came into the house after hauling an emergency supply of feed to the livestock.

Eugene was bundled up in a sheepskin coat, a billed cap with flaps that came down over his ears and tied under his chin, and five-buckle overshoes pulled on over his boots. Still he was cold. The thermometer on the post outside the back door stopped registering at minus thirty degrees. A strong north wind blew blizzard conditions.

They experienced one of those killer South Dakota blizzards that blasted through at least once--if not two or three times--each winter. It brought virtually all outside activity to a standstill.

These blizzards lasted anywhere from three days to a week. Horizontal winds piled huge drifts of snow across highways. Sometimes they trapped unwary travelers in their cars where they froze to death. Thousands of livestock were lost when they were driven against the fences by the wind, and the farmers couldn't get feed to them.

Anticipating the coming storm, Eugene strung a length of rope from the house to the barn, another from the barn to the cow shed. With winds up to fifty miles an hour and driving snow, everything turned white. A man could barely see beyond the length of his arm. It was easy to get disoriented and head off in the wrong direction to certain death.

Eugene said if it hadn't been for that rope to hang onto, he never would have made it out to the livestock shed and back again. One winter, Harold Weaver, who lived just a few miles down the road, got lost in a storm. The next day his family found him frozen in the snow within fifty yards of his own house.

The Alexander house was heated only by a single wood-burning, pot-bellied stove in the living room. At five-thirty every morning Eugene rousted out of bed, wearing only woolen socks and long-handled underwear. He'd go into the living room and start the fire. Some mornings, he would have to crack through the ice in the water bucket to fill the coffee pot. Then he'd go back and get dressed. Within a few minutes, the stove would be so hot that its sides glowed red and the coffee would be boiling. Thus fortified with a cup of freshly-brewed, scalding-hot coffee, Eugene would head on out to do the morning chores. The rest of the family stayed bundled up in bed until the house got warm.

Eugene delighted in telling a story about his brother Millard. It seems that Millard, like Eugene, wore his long-johns while lighting the stove. One particular morning, he got a roaring fire going and, still half-asleep, leaned back to stretch his muscles. But he was standing too close to the fire. He bumped against the red-hot stove, his fly popped open, and he severely burned his tallywhacker.

In winter the front room was closed off to save fuel except when we had company. The bedrooms weren't heated either, although there was a vent going up through the ceiling to allow a little heat to escape to the upstairs rooms.

Catherine and I slept upstairs in the same bed to stay warm. We slept in our clothes under a stack of four or five heavy quilts. It got so cold some nights the urine in our chamber pot froze solid. If it were a particularly cold night, Mom might fix a jar of hot water, wrap it in a towel, and place it under our feet to warm the bed. Come morning, that was frozen too.

My toes would get cold with the first snow in October and wouldn't warm up again until the March thaw.

Catherine and I got a special treat after one winter storm. The sky had cleared. The ground was covered with ice. The temperature was below zero.

Dad saddled up Fly, his riding horse, and hitched a rope to the saddle horn. The other end he tied onto our wooden sled. Then, with me and Catherine seated on the sled, he towed us around the snow-packed barnyard. Sometimes he had Fly go real fast, turn her sharply like a cutting horse, and cause the sled to swing in a wide, sweeping arc.

I thought that was about the most fun I had ever had. When it was time to quit I begged for more.

The locals had a favorite expression for the cold winters in South Dakota. "The only thing that stands between Artesian and the North Pole is two barbed wire fences."

About the only social activity during those long winter months was card-playing. Everyone played a version of whist called *Five Hundred*. I looked forward to these parties because there would always be other kids to play with.

We were over at the Olson's for a card party one night when the outside temperature dropped below zero and was getting colder. Dad expressed concern as to whether or not he would be able to get his car to start. Ole Olson showed him what to do. A half-hour before time to leave, Ole got an empty number 2 tin can, punched a ring of holes just under the top rim and poured it half-full with kerosene. They went out and slipped it under the car's oil pan and lit it with a match.

"I wouldn't take a brass monkey out in weather like this," Dad wisecracked as they came back inside to finish the card game. Nevertheless, by the time Dad and Mom were ready to leave for home, the kerosene fire had done its duty. The car's engine was warm enough to start.

One of the biggest hazards to winter driving was caused not by snow and ice on the road but by a thick coating of frost that froze on the insides of the windows. It was almost impossible for the driver to see where he was going. This frost was caused by the body heat of the passengers, combined with their moist breath, which froze on the car windows and built up opaque layers of the white stuff.

Dad's Model-A lacked a heater strong enough to defrost the windshield. To offset this problem, he--like most other car owners--bought little four-by-six-inch panels of glass which he mounted on the driver's windshield and side window. These panels, when sealed by an air-tight gasket, had the effect of creating a double pane of glass that resisted frosting over. This afforded a narrow slit through which he could peer ahead and to the side.

Nighttime driving was even worse. Dad bought a little rubber-bladed fan with a suction cup to mount on the dashboard to circulate air against the windshield. It helped, but not much. During really cold weather, the suction cup wouldn't stick. It was my job to hold the fan and point it in the right direction. But even if the fan and the glass panel were working right, Dad still had to drive with his body scrooched up over the steering wheel with his nose to the windshield. He did his best to see where he was going in the dim light of the Model-A's feeble headlamps.

One night as we drove back from Artesian, a strong crosswind blew wispy tendrils of snow across the road. Dad failed to recognize a three-foot snowdrift that had built up at the bottom of a swale. The car slammed into the drift with such force it got stuck in snow above the running boards.

Cursing vehemently, Dad got out the scoop shovel and tried to dig the car out. He got up front and pushed while Mom revved up the engine and tried to back out of the snow. But it wouldn't budge. Its forward motion had carried it so far into the snow bank that the wheels couldn't get traction. Finally, despairing of getting the car free, they wrapped themselves in blankets and the whole family huddled together in the back seat for warmth while waiting for daylight to come. Come morning, Dad hiked a half-mile back up the road to a farmhouse, where the farmer came down with a team of horses to pull the car free.

At other times when we were only going to be traveling a short distance--say, down to the next farm or over to Grandpa's house--it was easier to hitch up a team to the farm sled than to crank up the car. Dad's sled was actually a farm wagon that had the wheels replaced by sled runners.

When the sled was used as family transportation, Dad would toss a layer of straw in the wagon bed to cushion the ride. We all would pile in under a bunch of quilts to keep us warm. Except for Dad, that is. He had to sit up on the seat exposed to the weather.

Sometimes we sang and told stories. Other times we fell asleep or just rode in silence. On those nights when the sky was clear, we had a wonderful ride under the stars. The only sounds were snow crunching under the runners, leather creaking on the harness, and the clip-clop of horses' hooves.

Grandpa's Death

Diagnosed as having prostate cancer, Jesse Alexander moved into town in May of 1932. He no longer had the physical stamina to run his farm. He sold off the livestock and machinery at auction and let the land go back to the lender for the $16,000 owed against it.

Grandpa and Grandma's new home was a modest four-room bungalow two blocks west of Main Street. It faced south, framed by a couple of tall elm trees. There was hardly enough room for all Grandma's belongings. Her upright piano took up almost one full wall of the cramped living room.

I looked forward to visiting them because they always seemed so proud to see me. The first thing I'd do is run in and begin pounding away on Grandma's piano. I had no idea of what music I was playing; just making the sounds and singing away at the top of my lungs brought me pure joy. The nicest thing was that Grandma never criticized or told me I was doing it wrong.

One Friday morning in July 1934, when I was four, we all piled into the family car for a trip to Woonsocket, the county seat. Dad had to get some papers signed for Grandpa. On the way, we had to stop by Grandpa's house to pick up the papers. Catherine and I insisted on taking a pair of six-week-old black-and-tan puppies to play with on the trip.

For the first time I could remember, Grandpa didn't come out to greet us when we arrived. He came out only as far as the front door--not even onto the porch. Up to then, no one had told me of Grandpa's health problem, that he was dying of cancer, but I sensed that the man was very weak, fragile and preoccupied.

"Grandpa, is something wrong?" I asked.

"Your Grandpa hasn't been feeling well," he said to me.

"Will you get better soon?"

"Yes, I will get better soon," Grandpa said. That seemed to satisfy my curiosity for the moment.

Grandma suggested, "James, why don't you stay here and keep Grandma and Grandpa company while your mother and father go on to Woonsocket? Then they can pick you up on the way back home. Wouldn't you rather stay here with Grandma and Grandpa?"

I said I would.

A little while later, I was happily pounding away on the piano when Grandma came over to me. "James, your mother and dad are leaving now, would you like to wave good-bye to them?"

The separation of seeing Mom, Dad, Catherine, and Dick all get into the car and go off without me produced a great anxiety. My lip began to tremble and tears welled up in my eyes. "I want to go," I wailed, pulling away from Grandma.

She restrained me. "But don't you want to stay with Grandma and Grandpa? You said you would stay here with us." Her voice sounded hurt.

"No, I want to go!" I continued to scream and wail as only a four-year-old can.

Finally, Dad got back out of the car and came around to where I was standing. He picked me up and shook me to get me to stop crying. "Now stop being such a big baby," he demanded, dragging me over to the car and shoving me into the back seat.

"I hope you're satisfied!" Dad snarled as he drove off. "You made your grandmother feel bad, and she's never going to want to see you again."

I puckered up and cried again. In a little while, though, I forgot all about the episode and began picking on Catherine.

That was the last time I can remember seeing my grandfather alive.

Woonsocket, a town of 2,000 named by early settlers after a Rhode Island town of the same name, lay 19 miles west of Artesian on Highway 34. Dad wheeled into the parking lot behind the courthouse and left me and Catherine in the back seat of the car while he and Mom went inside to take care of whatever papers had to be signed. Seven-month-old Dick was sleeping on the front seat.

"You kids be good now, and don't wake up your brother," Mom said. She promised, "We'll be back in just a few minutes and buy you some ice cream."

The temperature on this July day was over 100 degrees--hotter inside the car. Catherine and I grew restless. For lack of something better to do, we busied ourselves with playing with the puppies we brought along. They were real cute.

At one point I laid back on the seat, stuck my bare feet out the window, and held the male puppy above my head. The dog began to urinate. The stream of warm pee hit me right in the mouth. I dropped the dog, yanked open the door, and ran behind the car to spit out the urine. I spit and spit, but no matter how hard I spit I couldn't get rid of the awful taste.

When Mom and Dad got back to the car, Catherine couldn't wait to tell them what happened. "Mom, Mom, guess what? James was playing with the dog, and the dog peed all over him."

I glared at her and silently vowed to get revenge.

Dad drove to the ice cream parlor. Mom went in to buy a pint of her favorite ice cream, maple walnut. We ate it in the car going down the highway. We handed the cardboard container back and forth, sharing the same spoon, until the delicious treat was all gone.

Catherine asked, "Mom, what do you want me to do with the box?"

"Just throw it out the door," Mom told her, not realizing Catherine would open the door of a moving vehicle. She assumed Catherine would toss it out the window. However, she didn't allow for the three-year old mind, which tends to take these commands quite literally. Thus when Mom said, "out the door," that's exactly what Catherine heard--"out the door."

Dick was wedged on the back seat next to the door on the passenger side, Catherine was in the middle, and I sat behind the driver. Catherine reached across Dick to turn the handle. On this particular model, the rear door opened from the front. There was no safety latch.

The door jerked wide open into a powerful stream of onrushing air. The wind caught Dick and began to suck him out the fast-moving car. Quicker than humanly possible, Mom's arm shot out and grabbed him as he was falling. If she had been a fraction of a second slower, the baby would have been tumbling down the paved highway at fifty miles an hour.

Dad skidded the car to a stop and walked around to close the door. His hand was shaking when he reached for the handle. Mom rocked back and forth in her seat, cuddling Dick, and saying over and over again, "I don't know why I looked around when I did. Something told me to." Catherine was crying in the back seat, afraid she was going to get fussed at. But Mom didn't blame her.

I marveled at how fast my mother could move in an emergency.

Jesse Alexander died on August 11, less than a month after the Woonsocket episode. I was four-and-a-half. The funeral was postponed until the 15th to allow time for his other sons to make the long trip from Iowa.

August in South Dakota is hot. Very hot. Dad joked it was so hot he woke up one morning to find that all the corn in the fields had popped, making him think it had snowed during the night.

The day of Grandpa's funeral was one of the hottest days of the year. The Artesian Methodist Church was like an oven inside. It was a white frame, L-shaped building built in 1886, measuring 26 x 50 feet, located just off town center. By 1928 its original congregation of sixty people had withered away to the point that the church was forced to close its doors. It reopened in November 1929 when Everett W. Palmer, a student at South Dakota Wesleyan University at Mitchell, agreed to come out on weekends to preach. He stayed until 1933. The little church seated seventy people when full.

The pews were rarely full except at weddings and funerals. A lot of townsfolk regularly turned out for funerals because that was one of the few forms of social entertainment in the area.

I was seated on the front row with Dad and his brothers Harry, Merlin and Millard. Womenfolk sat on the pew behind. This was the first time I can remember seeing Dad wear a suit. He looked uncomfortable in it.

The wooden pews were hard and sticky in the summer heat. I had to be reminded several times to sit still.

At the front of the church, between the pews and the pulpit, was Grandpa's coffin. I had never been to a funeral or seen a coffin before. I didn't grasp what it all meant. The casket was open. Grandpa looked like he was asleep. Several times I asked Dad why Grandpa was in there, but Dad told me to shush.

The new minister seemed uncomfortable and unsure of himself. He, like Reverend Palmer before him, was a college student who just came out on weekends. He had been on the job only two months. As things turned out, this was his first funeral. He plodded through the ritual in a nervously high pitched, sing-song voice.

When it was over, everyone filed past the coffin. Dad and his brothers led the way. Dad held me up to give me one last look at Grandpa.

We were guided into a small side room off the vestibule while the other mourners paid their final respects to Jesse. The tiny room had no windows, and it was unbearably hot. The men were sweating profusely in their suits and ties.

I asked Dad, "What are they going to do to Grandpa?"

"They're going to take him back to Iowa for burial."

I didn't really grasp the concept of death. "Will he come back and see us sometime?"

Dad choked up, unable to talk.

Uncle Harry, Dad's oldest brother, took over. "Your Grandpa is dead," he said. "He will never be able to come back to see you. You'll never see him again. Just remember how he looked the last time you saw him."

At that, the enormity and finality of the separation closed in on me. I began to cry. "I want to see Grandpa again," I sobbed.

"No, you can't see your Grandpa again."

I made an awful ruckus. I kicked and screamed, "I want to see Grandpa. I want to see Grandpa!"

They were unable to quiet me down. Finally, Uncle Merlin went to the undertaker and talked him into opening the coffin again. Dad carried me down to the front of the church where I got to see my Grandpa one more time.

"Say Good-bye to Grandpa, now," Dad told me.

"Good-bye, Grandpa," I said. I seemed satisfied.

On the fourteenth day of April
in nineteen thirty five,
There struck the worst of dust storms
that ever fill the sky;
You could see that dust storm coming,
it looked so awful black,
And through our little city,
it left a dreadful track.
From Oklahoma City
to the Arizona line,
Dakota and Nebraska
to the lazy Rio Grande,
It fell across our city
like a curtain of black rolled down,
We thought it was our judgment,
We thought it was our doom.
It covered up our fences,
it covered up our barns,
It covered up our tractors
in this wild and windy storm.
We loaded our jalopies
and piled our families in,
We rattled down the highway
to never come back again.
--"The Great Dust Storm"
--Woodie Guthrie

Dust Bowl Years

Grandpa's death was just the trigger, it wasn't the cause. My father's world began coming apart. The magnificent venture he had started with such high hopes in 1930 was now, in 1934, disintegrating into a house of shattered dreams.

I wasn't old enough to perceive the changes that were taking place in my world. For me, a four-year-old with no cares or responsibilities, life seemed pretty much as before.

Dad's spirit suffered a devastating psychological blow after Grandpa's death. Although his brothers never said so directly, they hinted that if Grandpa had been in Iowa where he belonged instead of up here with "Baby Gene," he could have received prompt and adequate medical care. They blamed Grandpa's death on Dad. Imagined or real, Dad keenly felt an undercurrent of resentment.

The real causes of Dad's tribulations were two factors beyond his control--the Dust Bowl and the Great Depression. The combined effects of depression and drought in the plains states brought South Dakota's economy to a standstill.

The Dust Bowl was not limited to Kansas, Nebraska and Oklahoma. It included the Dakotas, Wyoming, Colorado, eastern New Mexico, and the Texas panhandle.

The year 1930 saw a drought centered largely in the states east of the Mississippi, but its effects spilled over into the plains states as well. Farmers feared they would be forced to dispose of their breeding stock because of feed shortages and lack of money. In September 1930, the Farm Bureau reported six out of seven farm families would need assistance. One distressed farmer complained, "Congress seems to have plenty of money to bail out the banks, and only hell for the poor hungry farmers." Dad was better off than most because he grew his own feed and had plenty of water.

But the drought of 1930 was not taken seriously. In the following year, the greatest crop in the history of the region allowed farmers to forget their previous year's misfortunes. The glut of wheat in the marketplace caused a drop in wheat prices which, in turn, placed the plains farmers in a precarious financial position. In 1931 a bushel of No. 1 hard wheat sold for only twenty-seven cents at the farm.

If one were to select an arbitrary date for the first year of the

Dust Bowl it would be 1932. South Dakota received less than half its normal rainfall. A total of fourteen major dust storms were recorded in the Artesian/Sanborn County vicinity that year. Before the end of September, many of the farmers were unable to borrow money to pay their taxes. In Sanborn County, the only increase on the county's records that year was in the percentage of tax delinquencies. Nevertheless, there came a little rain late in the season that gave the farmers modest hope the drought was over. Most lived by the motto, "All we need is a little bit of rain."

The 1933 season began worse than the year before. Less than a quarter of an inch of rainfall was recorded for the entire month of April. The three-month total for May, June and July was only .64 of an inch. An excessive heat wave further added to the farmers' suffering.

Dust storms started with the coming of the new year. Two severe storms hit the area in the last half of May. One stirred up such great clouds of dust it was dangerous for cars to drive on the highways. The storm left a three-inch layer of sand on the lawns and created small sand dunes by sides of buildings.

The storms increased in number and intensity during the summer months. By the end of August, Artesian had witnessed more than thirty storms. One estimate placed the amount of topsoil lost by the average farm at two inches.

The dust was so fine-grained there was no way to keep it out of houses. It got on everything, in everything, and through everything. Even the food tasted gritty. Each morning, Mom woke up to find little mounds of dirt under the windows and doors where it had blown in during the night.

Despite the times, people maintained a sense of humor. They laughed, bitterly perhaps, because nature played a trick on them. They referred to the storms as "Black Blizzards" and "Sideways Tornadoes."

Tall tales abounded. A neighbor lady said she saw a hog with a bucket over his head running around the lot. She said she called it to her husband's attention. He, however, informed her that the hog was purposefully putting his head in the bucket to keep the sand out of his eyes.

Not to be outdone, Dad claimed the wind blew away so much of his soil that the postholes were left standing above the ground. He said he hitched up a team and wagon and went out and gathered up those postholes, and stored them in the barn for next year.

Worsening Drought

If people thought 1933 was a picture of disaster, 1934 became even worse. The third year of the drought brought a momentary hope that more favorable weather conditions might be returning. Snow cover that winter was fifty percent heavier than normal. After the spring run-off ended, however, it became evident there was not enough water to bring the desired results. The summer continued hot and dry. With 102-degree temperature before spring was officially over, the farmers of Sanborn County despaired of bringing in any crops. On scores of farms, bones of cattle which had died from starvation and thirst lay bleaching in the blazing sun. Stockyards were crammed with scrawny steers bought hastily by the government to aid stricken farmers.

The year ended with the drought still unbroken. As in the previous year, dust storms continued their work of destruction. Sand blew so thick people lost their way. Hens went to roost at midday. Farm wives kept lamps burning all day. Highway travel slowed to a crawl or stopped.

The big storm of May seventeenth and eighteenth caused a family living near Grandpa's old house to lose their way within one mile of home. The Herman Vogel family of four were driving a team northward when the storm swept down from that direction. This caused the horses to turn west away from the force of the storm. The Vogels, still thinking they were headed northward, lost their bearings. Herman got out of the wagon and found a fence line. He led the horses by hand along the fence until they came to a neighbor's house where they spent the night.

Still, Dad was not ready to give up. He kept his courage. He continued doing the things he had been trained to do, which was work his fields. He planted seeds in the dust just as though rainfall was ample and conditions ideal. It was an exercise in futility. He got heat stroke for his efforts. His corn didn't "head out" and had to be cut for silage. The wheat and oats were uprooted and blown away by the winds.

The smattering of rain that came late in summer was enough to sustain his faith that better times lie ahead. He greased his machinery, mended the fences, and made preparations for better times which he believed were certain to return. He felt they had endured the worst of the drought and the dust and 1935 was going to be the turn-around year in their fortunes.

The year 1935 was the worst year of the Dust Bowl. That year, Dad planted crops three times. Each time the seeds were blown away by the wind. His lungs were so filled with dust he developed a perpetual cough and spit black sputum.

April fourteenth produced the "mother of all storms." This monster storm of wind and dust, traveling at speeds up to sixty miles per hour, swept across the entire great plains region. It pushed southward from the Dakotas through Nebraska and Kansas. It left dust and devastation over a region that extended from Denver on the west and Iowa on the east, and south to the Texas Panhandle.

People who thought they had endured the worst that nature could throw at them looked in awe, many in terror. The advancing dust cloud had the appearance of a mammoth waterfall in reverse. It left the people stunned. They had never been in such an all-enveloping blackness before, such impenetrable gloom. In a moment, a bright Sunday afternoon was changed into darkness worse than midnight.

In Garden City, Kansas, it reduced visibility to zero. A businessman lost his way trying to crawl half a block to his home. When he recognized his location he was a whole block from his desired destination. At Liberal, Kansas, traffic on the highways was at a standstill because of drifting sand. Some cars stalled because of short-circuits in their electrical systems.

Near Colby a Rock Island train was derailed by dust drifts on the tracks. Another locomotive was derailed at Scott City, Kansas. Passenger trains on the main line of the Santa Fe stalled at Dodge City and Syracuse because the sand drifted over the tracks faster than section hands could shovel it off.

Through it all, people managed to invent "graveyard" stories which helped to keep up their courage. According to one of these stories, a man was on the highway out of Dalhart, Texas, when he was caught in the storm. When the wind subsided, he saw a man's hat on top of a brand-new sand dune. Upon investigating it he found a man's head to be underneath. He moved a little dirt from around the head and offered to help the man extricate himself. To this offer, the victim replied, "I don't think that's necessary. I'm on a tractor, and by tomorrow the wind will come from the other direction and blow the sand away so I can drive out."

According to another story, one farmer devised a new method for determining weather conditions. He would tie a long heavy chain to a post about four feet above the ground. If the wind blew hard enough to straighten the chain, the farmer knew it was too windy to work in his fields. Then he and his family would go visiting.

Another farmer reported that he saw "a prairie dog 100 feet in the air, burrowing."

The Last Year

Dad's cough worsened throughout the summer, and Mom got pregnant again. The baby, due in April, would be her fourth child in six years.

At first, Dad insisted his cough would go away when the dust storms stopped. But he began to experience headaches, malaise and muscle pains. Sometimes he would come from the fields in the middle of the day to take a rest. He complained of tiredness most of the time. By September, however, he was complaining of severe chest pains.

Mom knew it was serious. She talked him into going to see Doctor Loring.

Dr. Loring ordered Dad to bed immediately and told him he had to stay there for at least six weeks. He explained the situation to Mom. He said Eugene had contracted a form of pneumonia called *hypersensitive pneumonia*. He said it was very similar to *silicosis*, the coal miner's disease. It was caused largely by the collection of dust in the lungs. Other names for the illness were "dust pneumonia" and "dry pneumonia." He noted that the disease was showing a marked increase in the plains states, along with other respiratory ailments, because of the amount of dust in the air.

In an effort to impress Mom with the seriousness of the situation, Dr. Loring said, "I don't want to alarm you, but just five days ago the newspapers reported a produce truck driver at Elkhart, Kansas, had died with what the coroner described as dust pneumonia."

Of course, that did alarm Mom. She promised to restrain Dad from taking unnecessary chances with his health.

It fell upon Lillian--now twenty-three years old, with three kids already and a fourth on the way--to provide for her family's physical needs as well as nurse a sick husband back to health.

Winter was coming on, and the wood supply was low. Dad was in no condition to cut timber. In desperation, Mom bundled up us kids, hitched the wagon, and drove off across the prairie to pick up dried cow chips to burn for fuel. Dick, being too young to walk, rode on the wagon seat. Catherine and I trudged alongside Mom and helped her fill the wagon with chips.

Things got so bad Mom ran out of flour and did not have money to buy more. Being resourceful, she sent me out to the barn to run corn through the grinder. This hand-crank machine was intended to grind feed for cattle, not people. But it would have to do. I ground up a half-bushel at a batch, then took an old piece of screen wire and sifted the coarse granules out to get fine meal for Mom to use for cooking. We ate a lot of cornmeal mush, cornmeal pancakes, and corn bread.

Dad got well enough in November to get out of the house and do a few light chores. For a while it seemed that things were getting better.

Then another catastrophe struck. Hard up for money, Dad drove thirty miles north to Huron, a town of 15,000, to try to find work as a day laborer. His effort came to naught.

On his way home, the car caught fire. It seems that when Dad parked the car in Huron he laid a blanket across the top of the engine to keep the motor warm, thus making it easier to start in sub-zero weather. He forgot to remove the blanket when he started back. The carburetor apparently backfired and set the blanket on fire, which in turn burned up the electrical wiring. He just left the car on the side of the road and started walking. A passing motorist picked him up and brought him the rest of the way home. Dad went back with a team of horses the next day to tow the car home, but it was beyond repair.

That may have been the final straw. Dad had done a lot of thinking. He came to the hard realization it was pointless to go on this way. It would be a bitter pill to swallow, but there was no alternative. His money was gone, his health was impaired, his dreams were shattered, and his spirit was broken.

In December 1935, Eugene Alexander made the hardest decision he had ever made in his life. He wrote a letter to his brother Harry. He asked Harry to come up to South Dakota to get us. The ultimate indignity was that Dad no longer owned a car and thus lacked the means to get out of South Dakota on his own.

One task remained, and that was for Dad to sell off his remaining cattle. But there were no buyers. He offered to give them away. No one came forward. He even offered to help load them if anyone would take them. Still no takers.

He couldn't bear to watch his beloved steers starve. But other farmers were in the same fix. No one could afford to feed cattle for which there was no market. Tears came to his eyes when he turned them loose to fend for themselves on the open range.

Uncle Harry came up from Iowa in mid-January, bringing with him Uncle Millard, Dad's middle brother. They drove separate cars. Millard was towing a rubber-tired, four-wheel farm trailer.

Harry offered an observation. "For every truck we saw going into South Dakota, we saw ten leaving the state." He chuckled, apparently implying that Dad was not alone in having to leave the state under humiliating circumstances. Dad laughed painfully. It was small consolation.

They piled goods as high as the trailer would allow. When the vehicle would hold no more, they tied other cherished items into bundles and lashed them atop the cars. Whatever didn't fit either the trailer or car top got left behind.

By abandoning his farm implements, Dad was, in effect, leaving behind the tools of his trade. He gave up the means of earning a living as an independent farmer. Without implements with which to farm, he now would be relegated to working on other people's farms as a hired hand.

I rode in Harry's car with Dad, sitting in the middle with my feet astraddle the gear shift. The car's back seat was packed so high with household goods that Harry could barely see out the rear window. Catherine and Dick rode with Mom in Millard's car, which was also towing the overloaded trailer.

The weather was cold and the roads icy. The trailer slid off the road several times, necessitating numerous unplanned stops.

Moreover, Millard's car had no heater. Catherine complained of freezing to death in the back seat. She was told to wrap herself in another blanket. It was already noon when they passed Sioux Falls and crossed the Missouri River into Iowa. Mom asked hopefully, "Do you think we should stop at the next restaurant?"

Catherine thought, *Oh, how wonderful. Maybe I can get warm.*

But Millard was determined to make the trip in one day. No time for meal stops. "Oh no," he told her. "We can just make a baloney sandwich."

Catherine cried quietly.

It was thus that the Alexander family departed the land of the Dakotas.

They used to tell me I was building a dream,
And so I followed the mob--
When there was earth to plough or guns to bear
I was always there--right there on the job.
They used to tell me I was building a dream
With peace and glory ahead--
Why should I be standing in line
Just waiting for bread?
Refrain:
Once I built a railroad, made it run,
Made it race against time.
Once I built a railroad,
Now it's done--
Brother can you spare a dime?
Once I built a tower, to the sun.
Brick and rivet and lime,
Once I built a tower,
Now it's done--
Brother, can you spare a dime?
--"Brother, Can You Spare a Dime?"-1932

5

Hard Times

Winter of '36

Our rag-tail caravan drove through the night without rest. We arrived at Uncle Harry's house in Indianola the wee morning hours of Wednesday, January 22, 1936. Overall, we averaged barely twenty-five miles per hour over the four-hundred-fifty mile route. Most of the journey was plagued by ice, snow and freezing roads. Catherine and I were both asleep when we got there and barely roused when menfolk carried us into the house.

Indianola was a county-seat town of three thousand people.

Located just twenty miles south of the state capitol at Des Moines, it served, in some respects, as a bedroom community for its much larger neighbor to the north.

Indianola was also the home of Simpson College, a Methodist-related school named after Bishop Matthew Simpson of Civil War fame. Simpson College achieved renown as being the first American college to break the racial barrier. The famed black educator, George Washington Carver, enrolled there in 1890. It was the only college that would consent to admit a Negro.

My family's connection to that noteworthy event can be linked to my great aunt, Carrie Hawes, Grandpa Gamble's sister. She lived in the house previously owned by the lady who took Carver in. That kindly soul allowed the destitute but ambitious young black to sleep in her stable in exchange for doing odd jobs around the house.

The city's landscape was typical of a county-seat town. The center of activity was the county courthouse. Except for a few cafes and gas stations strung out along the highway, all the major stores and businesses were concentrated around the courthouse square.

My first few days in Indianola seemed like a blur. Each of us kids was parceled out to a different relative. I was sent to stay with Aunt Florence and Uncle Raymond Maxwell on their farm west of town. Catherine went with Uncle Millard and Aunt Wanda down to their farm at Milo, twelve miles southeast. And Dick was taken in by Uncle Merlin and Aunt Alta, who now lived on Grandpa's old farm. (They had bought it back from the bank for about ten cents on the dollar after it was foreclosed.)

The first thing Aunt Florence did when she got me in the house was give me a bath. Gosh knows how long it had been since I'd had one. She heated water in a boiler on top of the wood-burning kitchen range, poured it into the tub of her Maytag washing machine, and dumped me into it. After giving me a thorough scrubbing, she then used the same water to wash my grungy clothes. Meanwhile, she outfitted me in some clean hand-me-down clothes that her son, Dale, five years older than me, had outgrown.

Aunt Florence also had a daughter, Faune, who was two years older than me. I didn't get to meet my cousins until later in the day because they were at school while all this cleanup was going on.

Dale was learning to play the trombone. He made it look so easy that I was sure I could do it too. I begged him to let me try. But I couldn't get my mouth puckered right. Instead of music, all I got was a sound much like the moan of a sick calf.

With Dale and Faune away at school every day, there wasn't anyone for me to play with. I got so homesick for the rest of my family that I followed Aunt Florence around, constantly underfoot. I talked incessantly, telling her everything I had ever learned or thought about. At first, Aunt Florence seemed amused by it, but after hearing so much chatter her patience began to grow thin. Time after time, she said to me, "Now, James, I want you to sit in that chair, and I want you to keep quiet for the next half hour." I never succeeded in going a whole half hour without talking. Five or ten minutes at a time was the best I could do.

My sixth birthday was coming up on February 16. Uncle Raymond promised to drive me into town so I could celebrate it with Mom and Dad. Naturally, I was excited about the trip and could hardly wait to see my parents again.

Unfortunately, the morning of the fifteenth blew in a big snow storm which brought all travel to a standstill. Uncle Raymond cautioned, "I don't know if we're going to be able to make it tomorrow or not."

There was no let-up on the sixteenth. The storm blew for another three days, and huge snowdrifts blocked all county roads. Aunt Florence did what she could to make this a happy birthday for me. She baked me a cake and wrapped some presents. But it wasn't quite the same as being with my own mother and father.

After the storm subsided, the sun came out and created a beautiful, snow-covered rural scene. Uncle Raymond hitched a team of horses to a sled. We started the four-and-a-half miles into town. About a mile-and-a-half down the road we passed a county snowplow that was completely buried in a snowdrift. Only the very top of its yellow cab showed above the snow.

Uncle Millard arranged for Dad to get a temporary job with the WPA down in Milo. "WPA" stood for Works Progress Administration. It was a Roosevelt program designed to give out-of-work, Depression-era people a job building public improvement projects like roads, bridges and lakes.

Dad was hired to help build a concrete bridge across a creek to replace an old wooden one. He found himself running a horse-drawn road scraper much like the one he used to build the pond on his farm in South Dakota. The job was expected to last only three months or so, and the pay wasn't very much, but at least it gave Dad a way to put food on the table without taking handouts.

Millard made a deal with some nearby neighbors, the Biddles, whereby Dad could move his family into a vacant farm house in exchange for doing chores. With Millard's help, we moved our meager belongings down from Indianola on the first weekend in March 1936.

Shirley's Birth

Mom was pregnant again for the fourth time. She kept a flat box approximately 24-inches by 24-inches under the bed. It contained baby clothes. Catherine, not quite five, was obsessed with the idea of having a new baby. She would pull the box from under the bed and show it to anyone who happened to come to visit. She'd tell people, "See, these are for Beverly Louise, the new baby." Mom would get embarrassed and try to make her put them back.

On Easter Sunday, which was April twelfth, Mom didn't get out of bed. Dad fixed breakfast and fed us kids--something very unusual for him to do. Pretty soon a doctor came to see Mom. A few minutes later he came out of the bedroom and spoke quietly with Dad, their heads almost touching. Dad came over to where

Catherine and I were playing and asked, "How would you kids like to go for a ride? Would you like to see the bridge your Dad has been working on?"

We eagerly chimed yes. Dad left Dick with Millard's wife, hitched up a team and drove down the road where the new bridge was taking shape. The dirt was freshly mounded up and wooden forms were ready to pour concrete. Mr. Biddle and his two grown sons soon came to join us. Dad went back to the house. Catherine and I clambered around in the dirt and climbed the concrete forms while the grownups talked.

Shortly before noon, Uncle Millard drove up in his Model-A Ford. Dad was with him. Dad stepped out of the car and called for Catherine and me to come over to the car. "How would you kids feel about having a little baby sister?" he asked.

Catherine squealed with delight and started jumping up and down. She clapped her hands with glee. As for me, I was un-moved by the news. I wanted to get back to playing on the mounded dirt.

Dad told us the new baby's name was going to be "Shirley Ann." Catherine seemed confused. She couldn't figure out what happened to "Beverly Louise." Later, she learned Dad decided at the last minute to name her Shirley, because Shirley Temple was all the rage.

Shirley was a round, roly poly, blue-eyed blonde, with dimples just like Shirley Temple's. The doctor told Dad that it would be sixty years before Shirley's birthday came around on Easter Sunday again.

Grandma Alexander came out to help around the house while Mom was recuperating. It was customary for a new mother to stay in bed for a week to ten days after delivery.

One day she sent Catherine and me out to dispose of a stack of newspapers. Catherine was in a fire-lighting stage. We carried the papers to the root cellar where our actions couldn't be seen. We lit the papers.

It wasn't much of a fire. Little actual damage was done, but thick smoke poured forth. Indeed, the residue of the smoke so coated Mom's jars of canned foods stored in the root cellar that she couldn't read the labels. Nor could she see the contents inside. Thereafter, whenever someone was sent to get a jar of tomatoes, he might come back with a jar of peas or something else.

That was Catherine's third fire in one week. Grandma Alexander couldn't handle it. She made Dad take her back to town.

Catherine also set Uncle Millard's car on fire. She lit a match and the fabric upholstery went "poof." The whole inside was scorched, but the outside was okay. She got her fanny tanned for that. I got it too, even though I hadn't done anything. Sometimes things worked out that way; I got paddled just on general principles.

Fourth of July

July Fourth was coming up and Mom told Catherine and me if we didn't light any more fires, we could have some fireworks.

I held up my end of the bargain, but Catherine didn't. On the very last afternoon before the Fourth, Mom sent Catherine out to the field with Dad's lunch pail. Catherine lit one more little fire.

"All right, young lady," Mom said, "No fireworks for you!" She gave her a little butt-warming, too.

When we all drove into town that Friday evening to buy fireworks--the Fourth being on Saturday--Mom made it clear to Catherine she wouldn't get any. Catherine reasoned that if they thought she was dying, they might feel sorry and give in. So she moaned and groaned and rolled around the back seat holding her stomach all the way to town. It didn't work. She got no fireworks.

Catherine and I both learned an important lesson: when Mom and Dad said we were going to get something (like a whipping)--or not get something--they stuck by their word and they never backed down. Catherine was never promised a whipping she didn't get. Sometimes she might have to wait until after supper, or maybe the next day or day after, but she could be sure that it was coming, and that it was hell waiting. The waiting was worse than the whipping.

I went out in the yard with my fireworks before breakfast the next morning. Dad was in the barn milking cows. Catherine had stay in the house and was only allowed to watch out the kitchen window. That pained her deeply, but this was part of her punishment.

There was a nice, bare patch of ground between the house and the barn where I could set off my firecrackers. For a while, I lit them one at a time. I would lay one of the "ladyfingers" on a rock, light it gingerly with a big kitchen match, and run off ten or fifteen feet before it exploded. I tired of that routine after a while, however, and decided to go in for bigger things. I laid a whole string of firecrackers on a flat rock and lit the fuse. They went off with a wondrous noise, sounding like a machine gun.

Dad came charging out of the barn with the front of his overalls covered with milk. His face was as red as a boiled lobster. He yelled, "What in God's name are you doing?"

Dad had been milking the cows. As long as my firecrackers went off one at a time, the cow would just give a little kick, and then Dad could go on milking. However, when I lit off the whole string, all hell broke loose in that barn. The cows started bucking and trying to escape from their stalls. That's when the bucket of milk got spilled all over Dad.

Grandma's Birthday

Grandma Gamble's fifty-fourth birthday was coming up on July sixth. Her kinfolk planned to celebrate it the day prior--Sunday the fifth. Each family was designated to bring a different dish. Mom volunteered to bake the cake.

This meant that Mom had to do her baking on Saturday, the fourth. As soon as Dad finished with his chores and got cleaned up, he drove Mom to Indianola. Then he took us children to the Fourth of July celebration at the park.

Mom worked all day to make an angel food cake on Grandma's wood-burning kitchen range. That was a tremendous feat, considering Mom beat 12 dozen eggs by hand. The bottom layer was baked in a foot tub, the second layer in a dish pan, the top layer in a standard angel-food cake pan. She decorated it in red, white and blue with little flags. Her cake was a thing of beauty.

All of the aunts and uncles were there. After the meal was over, everyone was relaxed in the front yard, taking pictures and visiting.

Catherine sneaked off to the outhouse and set a catalog on fire. She barely got the fire going when one of the uncles came out to use the outhouse. He discovered the fire. He grabbed her up and took her out into the yard, pulled down her panties, and in front of everybody tanned her little fanny. The whole episode caused quite a commotion and everybody came to look. The menfolk ran to get some buckets of water to douse the flames.

Catherine was so embarrassed she never lit another fire.

Gillett Grove

When the WPA job ended, Dad's boss said he had a job for him on another road-building project if he wanted it. It was near the town of Gillett Grove, two hundred miles to the northwest near Spencer. Dad went to look it over, came back, and told Mom they were moving. Mom cried at the thought of moving far away from her family again. Dad insisted this was his chance to get a fresh start.

Mom accused him, "Face the truth, the reason you want to move so far away is because you can't stand the idea of being around the people you grew up with, looking like a failure."

Nevertheless, with Uncle Millard's help, they hauled their belongings from Milo to Gillett Grove in mid-August of 1936.

Gillett Grove was a slowly decaying hamlet of about 150 people. It wasn't on the road to anywhere. Indeed, it was the kind of town time seemed to have passed by.

Dad had talked the owner of a vacant house into renting it to him on the promise he would pay as soon as he got his first paycheck. The owner had little choice. It was better to have a house lived in than for it to sit vacant and open to the ravages of wind and the weather.

Our new home was a small white house on the east side of Main Street directly across from the grain elevator. The house was difficult to keep clean because none of the town's streets were paved. Every time a car or truck passed by clouds of dust were kicked up into the air and borne into the house. The dust was especially bad on hot summer days when the streets were dry and windows and doors had to be kept open in the suffocating heat.

Catherine and I made friends with the man who ran the street grader. This was a tractor-like vehicle, painted bright yellow, that was long and low in the front with a high cab in the back. A big scraper blade ran crossways under the middle. Inside the cab, the operator had a bewildering array of cranks and levers that he manipulated to raise or lower the blade, adjust its angle, and rotate it from left to right. I was fascinated with how this wonderful piece of machinery worked.

Twice a week, the operator graded the streets and roads to even out the ruts and make the roadway smooth for travel. Sometimes he would let Catherine and me ride inside the cab. That was exciting. Other times, we would run up behind the moving machine and hitch a ride on the back step. If Mom caught us doing that, she would give us a swat and warn that it was dangerous. But it was such great fun that we did it anyway.

Dad's job didn't pan out. I never learned why. But Dad hired on with a farmer about three-fourths of a mile west of town to finish out the threshing season. Dad took the job no one else on the threshing crew wanted, stacking straw. That chore required him to stand directly in the stream of straw and chaff. He directed the straw into a well-molded, crescent-shaped stack ten feet high. It was incredibly dusty and suffocating work. He tied a red bandanna across his mouth to keep from breathing dust and wore a pair of goggles to keep the chaff out of his eyes. At the end of the day he was so caked with layers of sweat and grain dust he looked like a Kentucky coal miner.

The threshing season lasted a couple of weeks. When it ended, the farmer and his wife took pity on Dad's economic plight. They provided him what additional work they could afford. They paid him to do needed repairs around the farm and build a new addition to the barn.

Mom loved to sew, and she was good at it. One of her dearest possessions was her treadle sewing machine. Somehow, she had lugged it all the way up to South Dakota, back down to Indianola, over to Milo, and now up to Gillett Grove. She made all the kids' clothes as well as her own. One time she made a suit for Dad. Whenever she could find a customer--which wasn't often in this small community--she took in sewing to help put food on the table.

She kept her carefully-hoarded money in the little needle drawer on the side of the machine. The family's wealth was down to twelve cents, a dime and two pennies. Mom asked me to run down to the store and buy some Karo syrup for Shirley's formula. When she opened the needle drawer to get her money, she only found two pennies. The dime was missing. She searched frantically for that dime, turning the drawer upside down and pawing through its contents item by item.

She confronted me in a very accusatory tone, "Did you take that money? Don't lie to me, young man!"

Frightened at her anger, I stoutly protested.

Catherine came to my defense. She remembered a neighborhood boy had been over earlier that morning. "Maybe he took it," she offered hopefully.

Mom broke down in tears, sobbing uncontrollably in helpless frustration. "God damn," she stormed futilely, "up here in this god-forsaken place...(sob)...no money...(sob)...four mouths to feed and not a stick of food in the house...(sob). Somebody had the unmitigated gall to steal the last dime I had to my name. (sob) What's the use?"

My first day in school was a sharp disappointment. The school building was across the block to the east, less than a couple hundred feet away. It was a two-story, buff-colored brick building, with the elementary grades occupying the ground floor. The high school was on the upper level. Most of the students came to school by bus from surrounding farms.

Catherine and I started in the first grade together, even though I was a year older. With the problems they had in South Dakota and moving to Iowa, Mom and Dad had failed to enroll me in school before now. I was six-and-a-half.

First and second grades shared the same teacher. First-graders were on the right side of the room and second-graders on the left. One group was supposed to study while the other recited.

I had looked forward to the experience with great anticipation. I thought I was going to learn everything.

The teacher began the first lesson: "I'm going to teach you how to write your numbers," she said. She turned toward the blackboard. She made a big show of writing the numerals one, two, three, four, and five. She told a little story about each number to help the pupils remember it. Then she told them to practice writing those numbers while she taught the second-graders. After numbers they were allowed to color pictures with crayons. At noon, she sent them home for the day.

I felt let down. I didn't learn anything I didn't already know. For over a year I had been able to count past a hundred and recite the alphabet. I wanted to get on with the business of learning. To me, it was a waste of time to cut out, color and paste.

After two weeks, the teacher had a talk with Mom. She suggested they move me into the second grade. Mom talked to Dad, and they made the decision it might do more harm than good to move me ahead too fast. They kept me in the first grade with Catherine.

There was a girl in the second grade I fell head over heels in love with. Her name was Constance. I thought "Constance" was the prettiest name I had ever heard and she was the prettiest girl I had ever seen. Constance lived on a farm outside town and rode on the bus, so I only got to see her at school.

The budding romance ended when we moved away from Gillett Grove after the first six weeks of school. But I daydreamed about Constance for many months afterwards.

We have Hooverized on butter,
For milk we've only water,
And I haven't seen a steak in many a day;
As for pies, cakes, and jellies,
We substitute sow-bellies.
For which we work the county road each day.
Oh, those beans, bacon, and gravy,
They almost drive me crazy
I eat them till I see them in my dreams,
In my dreams;
When I wake up in the morning,
And another day is dawning.
Yes, I know I'll have another mess of beans.
--"Beans, Bacon, and Gravy"

6

The Hungry Years

Webb #1

Dad and Mom were forced to vacate the little house in Gillett Grove when the owner concluded they were never going to pay any rent. Dad found a place in the town of Webb, seven miles to the south. It was now mid-October 1936. Cold weather was setting in.

Dad still did not have a steady job, but his gift of gab remained undiminished. He hornswoggled a man named Freddie Tielbur into letting us move into an empty farm house that Tielbur owned on the east side of town. Tielbur, like many owners of vacant property during the height of the farm depression, was so desperate for tenants that he would take anyone on "a lick and a promise," so to speak.

The town of Webb was even smaller than Gillett Grove. Its

main reason for existing was the "Consolidated" school which took the place of numerous little country schools. In addition, there was a grain elevator, grocery store, and gas station. The sign across the top of the grain elevator read CO-OP. I doubt that more than fifty people lived there.

Dad hired out as a general laborer at a dollar a day. The work wasn't steady, but he managed to bring in enough money to feed his family.

The house set back from the road, facing east. It was reached by a long lane which curved south. The yard was overgrown with grass and weeds, many as tall as I was.

The tall grass made a wonderful place to play "Cowboys and Indians." One day our play came to a sudden halt when Catherine stepped on a rusty ten-penny nail. The point penetrated all the way through her foot and came out the top.

Mom never considered taking her to a doctor. For one reason, there wasn't any money. Besides, farm families were used to conducting their own remedies.

Instead, Mom pulled the nail out, doused the wound with generous amounts of turpentine, and soaked Catherine's foot in Lysol. Then she made a hot bread-and-milk poultice to put on it. For the next three days she changed the poultice every two hours and checked for tell-tale red streaks that would indicate blood poisoning. Fortunately, no red streaks appeared, and a week later Catherine's foot was as good as new.

Changing schools after only six weeks meant having to negotiate a whole set of new relationships. New teachers, new classmates, new setting. The Webb school was a two-story, L-shaped purple brick building one-and-a-half blocks east of town center. The high school occupied the west wing.

My classroom was on the second floor, north side. As in Gillett Grove, two grades were housed in the same room. The setting was much less formal. At the front was a circle of chairs. Whenever it was time for one of the grades to recite, the pupils would go up and sit in the circle. The wall beside the second graders held a chart showing all the phonics symbols. I quickly learned those I didn't already know.

Catherine had to sit next to a boy named Lail Potter, whom she didn't like. She said he smelled like he had peed his pants and wore them for three months at a time.

Miss Muller was our teacher. She pronounced her name as "Mewler," which rhymes with "mule"--the nickname by which kids called her behind her back. She was plain, thirtyish, wore round metal-rimmed glasses, and drew her ash-blonde hair into a bun on the back of her head.

During my first recitation period in the new school, Miss Muller held a wooden model of a clock with oversize numerals on it. Her aim was to teach the first-graders how to tell time. She showed us how the position of the big hand and little hand could tell them what time of day it was. I already knew that. I called out all the answers correctly.

Apparently I disrupted the other children's learning by blurting out all the answers myself, for Miss Muller handed me a book and told me to go back to my desk and look at the pictures while she finished the lesson. When she came back later to check on how I was doing, she found me reading the words. This was considered unusual for child with only six weeks of schooling, so she tested me on both reading and arithmetic and said I should really be in the second grade.

Again, Mom refused to go along with the idea of my skipping a grade. When Miss Muller asked why, Mom said she herself had skipped the third grade when she was in school and had always regretted it.

Miss Muller was not to be outdone, however. She quietly moved me to a desk next to the second grade side of the room and let me do second grade work. Nonetheless, I still only got credit for being in the first grade.

Sometimes when she didn't want to be bothered with questions from the kids, she'd say, "Ask James, he knows."

Mom groused, "I send him to school to learn, not to be a teacher."

Miss Muller read the story of Red Riding Hood and the Big

Bad Wolf in class. That story seemed so real to Catherine's impressionable mind that she became very fearful. She was sure that the Big Bad Wolf was real. It might be behind any rock or just over the hill. For several weeks she didn't venture out of doors by herself unless she absolutely had to.

It seemed that everybody wanted to pick on me. I don't know why, unless it was a crime to have red hair. I might as well have been from Mars. No matter who did something wrong, I got blamed. Everyone wanted to take a poke at me.

One blustery wintry day some of the bigger boys from the third and fourth grades taunted me at recess. They said only sissies had red hair. I got mad and spouted back at them. More boys chimed in. They formed a circle that penned me in like a caged animal. Desperately, I tried to fight my way out. They pushed me back into the center, made taunting remarks and tossed pebbles at me. I looked around frantically for a friendly face. There was no one to help me. No one dared. Finally, the bell rang signaling the end of recess, and the terrible ordeal was over as quickly as it began.

Back inside the safety of the classroom, the teacher took me aside. She said she had been watching out the window and saw the whole incident. I heaved a sigh of relief. I thought she was going to report my tormenters to the principal. The possibility of their punishment gave me satisfaction. Instead, she told me I was going to have to learn to control my temper, and as punishment she was going to make me stay after school for fighting.

Money was scarce. The family subsisted mostly on potatoes supplemented by vegetables Mom had canned in fruit jars. She learned a hundred ways to fix potatoes. Sometimes us kids didn't realize we were eating 'taters.

"We're so poor," Dad joked, "that the flies have to carry their own lunches when they come to our house."

One time Mom was down to only tomatoes in the pantry. Supper consisted of potatoes and a big mess of breaded tomatoes. But Catherine couldn't stand the taste of tomatoes. Mom told her, "If you don't like them, I won't force you to eat them. But there isn't anything else." So Catherine forced herself to eat them...take a bite, wash it down with water, take another bite, and so on.

But no matter how poor we were, Mom always found some way to finish off the meal with a dessert. It might be a cake without frosting, or bread pudding, but there was always something.

We had lots of homemade bread. Mom baked five loaves every second day. There wasn't any butter or jam to put on it, so we experimented using lard mixed with sugar. It tasted terrible.

Catherine, in particular, was embarrassed to take a lunch to school of just bread with nothing on it. She tried to turn away from the other kids so they couldn't see what she was eating.

One time Dad bought six slices of bologna for a nickel. Each member of the family got a slice--all except Shirley, of course, who was too little. Dad ate her slice. That bologna was delicious. Catherine said she never tasted anything that came close to being as good as that bologna.

Catherine started school with three dresses made of flour sacks. She wore one a week. Each day when she came home from school, she took her school clothes off and put on her overalls. She felt more at home being a tomboy.

Mom didn't have a washing machine. All the clothes had to be washed out by hand. She had a round, galvanized wash tub which she filled with water heated on top of the stove. She scrubbed the clothes up and down on a washboard. She wrung them out by hand and put them in a pile until she had done all the clothes. Then she'd lug that heavy tub of water out the back door and dump it out. Sometimes she'd give the kids a bath in the water before she poured it out. Then she refilled the tub with more water heated on the stove to rinse the clothes previously stacked up on the floor. Finally, she dumped the white things into a boiler on top of the stove to boil out the remaining soap.

The clothes were hung outdoors to dry on a clothesline. In winter months, they froze as stiff as boards.

Ironing clothes was another feat. Usually, Mom washed on Tuesdays and ironed on Wednesdays. She had three or four cast-iron irons which she heated on top of the stove. Each had a little handle that curved up on top. The handle usually got too hot to hold in bare hands, so Mom used pot holders. Getting the irons heated to just the right temperature was a delicate art. They started cooling as soon as she took them off the stove. That's why it was necessary to have three or four irons--as each cooled down she exchanged it for a hot one.

One wash day Catherine and I misbehaved and Mom didn't have time to fool with us. She made us go sit in chairs. She separated us by putting Catherine on one side of the room and me on the other.

Bored with inactivity, the two of us started throwing pillows back and forth at each other. One pillow broke and its feathers spilled out. About that time Mom poked her head around the corner to check on us; she saw the whole room covered with feathers. She threw a screaming fit.

Once in a while, a big box of used clothes would come from Indianola. Mom's relatives sent us their old suits, coats, and dresses. Mom would rip the seams apart, lay Catherine, Dick or me down on the material and draw around us. The next morning, she would have made a new item of apparel.

People say I had a sweet voice. Teachers often called upon me to sing at school functions. Most requested was, "God Bless America." There seemed to be something irresistable about a freckle-faced, red-haired kid singing at the top of his lungs--whether of not he stayed on key.

At the annual Christmas pageant, I played the lead role in my class's skit. The school's Christmas pageant was one that community's major social events of the season. Teachers and parents put a lot of effort into decorating the building and preparing the skits. I sang my heart out. At the finale, they brought me back on stage to sing "God Bless America."

Christmas in the Alexander household was rather skimpy that year because there was no money to buy presents. We had to make them.

Dad cut a tree which we decorated with popcorn strings and curly pieces of paper. Mom made a little table and chairs out of nail kegs for Catherine and me as our presents. Also, Catherine got her first doll. I fashioned a cradle for her doll out of wood from an egg crate. The only problem was the paint didn't dry and it stuck to the tissue paper I used to wrap the gift. Ultimately, that didn't matter, however, because Dick rocked over the doll's head the first day and broke it. Catherine didn't get upset; she was too much of a tomboy to care about dolls.

Catherine got an orange and a string of blue beads in her Christmas stocking. She liked them better than the doll.

Mom served Cream of Wheat on Christmas morning instead of the loathsome oatmeal.

The previous night, Mom put out a plate of fudge and cookies so Santa could have a snack. Apparently he ate the whole thing because there wasn't a scrap left on Christmas morning. Mom acted really put out and she ranted on and on about what a big pig Santa was.

January was hog-butchering time. Four or five farmers butchered at the Tielburs in a communal effort. The event was quite a festive occasion. The men told jokes while they butchered. The womenfolk boiled vats of water to scald the hogs. The kids ran around underfoot and made nuisances of themselves.

When the butchering was finished and the meat wrapped to take into the locker plant for freezing, the men washed up and trooped into the house. There they found food and beverages in abundance. There was beer and steaming coffee, thick slabs of fresh-from-the-oven bread, and fried slices of pork from newly-butchered pigs to make sandwiches.

There was a lot of joshing about who had the courage to eat one particular sandwich filling, namely, "Rocky Mountain oysters." That was a euphemism for the pig's testicles. Not one to be shy, on a dare I ate one of them on a sandwich. I found it to be quite tasty.

One man took a pig's tail, sliced it open, and placed it between two slices of bread. He offered a quarter to anyone who would take a bite of it. Dick, now three, was the only taker; but the guy reneged on giving him the quarter. That made Mom mad. She told the guy that was a dirty trick to play on a little kid.

Greenville

The traditional work year on Iowa farms ran from March first to March first, just in time for the spring planting season. In Iowa, every March first was a giant game of musical chairs. Those who changed jobs moved to their new locations on the same day.

March 1, 1937, found the Alexander family on the move again. Dad secured a job as hired hand on the El Ferdean farm near the town of Greenville.

Greenville, with a population of 220, formed a triangle with Webb and Gillett Grove. Each town was about seven miles from the other, with Greenville being the western point. All three were located in the southeastern corner of Clay County. The county seat was Spencer, some fifteen miles away at the geographical center of the county.

Elbert "El" Ferdean's farm lay two-and-a-half miles west of Greenville. The main farm itself, where the Ferdeans lived, was situated on the north side of the road. The hired hand's house, where we would live, was an eighth of a mile back towards town on the opposite side of the road. The property consisted of a smallish one-story house, a barn, machinery shed, and some outbuildings. In years past, this had been an independent farm.

Mr. Ferdean worked for the railroad. He ran the little puddle-jumper up and down the tracks to make sure they were clear before the train came through.

The Ferdean family had five children ranging from age fifteen down to one year. Two of the boys, Elbert, Jr. and Tommy, were eight and nine, respectively, just one and two years older than I.

The move to Greenville meant that Catherine and I were now enrolled in our third school of the year. Unlike Gillett Grove and Webb, we rode a bus to school each morning. Our bus was not very big. It carried a dozen kids who sat along the sides facing the middle, rather than on seats lined up in a row.

There was a fifth-grade girl, Darlene Richardson, who thought it was fun to tease me because of my red hair. She liked to make me blush. She'd slide up next to me and pretend to be madly in love with me. She might say something like, "Come and sit by me so we can hold hands," or, "Can I kiss you?" I was so embarrassed I would try to push her away. This caused the other kids to laugh and join in the merriment.

"James," Mom lectured me, "she's only teasing you because she knows you won't kiss her. The next time Darlene asks you, say yes. I'll bet she'll be so surprised that she'll stop teasing you."

Despite that advice, I never got up enough courage to test Mom's theory. Probably, I was secretly pleased by Darlene's attention.

House Fire

Our new home was ramshackle and run-down, having suffered many years of neglect. It was a long, low, row house with two bedrooms tacked onto the east end. Their only exit was through the living room. The kitchen was on the west end. A covered back porch opened off to the south.

The yellowish paint was faded and peeling. The dwelling had no second floor, but there was an attic where we kids loved to play. The chimney from the living room stove passed through the attic. There were so many chinks between the bricks that we could watch flames and sparks spiral upwards whenever Dad built a fire.

Dad made a down payment on a new Maytag washing machine. That made Mom happy. She still had to heat water on the kitchen stove, but at least she no longer had to wash clothes by hand.

Shirley's first birthday came on April twelfth. It had snowed a few days earlier. By now the snow was mostly gone but the temperature was still cold enough that there was frost on the ground.

Dad got up about four-thirty and lit a fire in the stove, as was his custom. He went down to the big farm to do the chores while the rest of the family stayed in bed.

The three of us older kids were sleeping in the north bedroom. Baby Shirley was with Mom in the other. Catherine's bed was against one wall, mine in the middle, and Dick slept in a crib against the other wall. Catherine had fallen asleep the night before while wearing a purple dress she hated. She was still in it.

Catherine woke up early, a little after five, and saw sparks drifting down at the foot of my bed. At first, she was too awestruck to do anything about it. She laid there and watched it, fascinated by the flames. *That's strange,* she thought. Finally, she got up and walked over to my bed and shook me awake.

My reaction time was swifter than hers. I came out of bed like a bullet, screaming, "Mom, the house is on fire!"

I lifted three-year-old Dick out of his crib. Mom grabbed Shirley, and we all ran through the living room and out the back door. Everyone was barefooted. Mom had on only her pink nightgown. Catherine still had on the purple dress she hated.

Mom parked everyone in the yard. Then she tried to go back in. But the flames consumed the house in almost no time. She could only get to the back porch. The first trip, she grabbed an armload of overalls for the boys and a sheepskin coat which she pulled on over her night gown. Then she went back in and, in what seemed like a superhuman effort, she grabbed her new Maytag washing machine in one hand and a hundred-pound sack of potatoes in the other. She dragged them both out into the yard.

The fire got so bad she couldn't go back in a third time. She moved us kids to the shelter of the barn.

Since there were no phones or fire trucks out in the country, there wasn't any way to save the house once it started burning. Neighbors saw the fire and reported it to the Ferdeans.

Dad knew his wife and children were still asleep in the house when he left. He became so hysterical thinking they had perished in the flames he had to be forcibly restrained. He broke down and cried when he found we were safe and unharmed in the barn.

Mr. Ferdean came running up the road carrying a stepladder and a pail of water. He watched helplessly a few minutes, then said, "get the lady and the kids out of there." Mom took us kids in tow and began walking down the gravel road toward the Ferdean's house. We were still barefooted. On a good day, it would have been bad enough walking barefoot on gravel, but on a frosty morning it felt like walking on chunks of glass. It hurt.

Down the road we went--Mom in her pink nightgown and sheepskin coat, carrying one-year-old Shirley. She tried to wrap the coat around Shirley to keep her warm. We three kids trailed behind. Dick was three, Catherine almost six, I was seven. The walk seemed much longer than an eighth of a mile. Catherine was mad that her brand new lunch box had burned up and all she saved was that hated purple dress.

For the next three months we camped upstairs at the Ferdean's house. There was an announcement on the radio about the fire and people came with boxes of clothes, dishes, and linens. In the end we may have had more goods after the fire than before.

The railroad track ran directly in front of the Ferdean's house. It never bothered us kids to walk along the tracks because we always knew when the trains came through. One day, however, we were unaware of an extra train coming through. Catherine, two of the Ferdean boys, and I were on a trestle over the river, tossing pebbles into the water. We didn't have a care in the world. We finished our play and started to mosey back towards the house. We noticed some grownups at the edge of the bridge, jumping up and down and waving their arms frantically. We couldn't hear what they were yelling, so we continued to mosey along unconcerned. When we got to the end of the trestle, our parents grabbed us and pulled us off the bridge. It was just in the nick of time. A train came roaring through.

Mom started paddling Catherine and me on our behinds. Catherine asked her, "Did you beat me because you were mad that I didn't get killed?"

Another time, Catherine and I were playing on the far side of the tracks. Dick was with us. A train was due to come along shortly. We asked Dick if he wanted to stay on the side with us or go back to Mom who was standing just a few feet on the other side of the tracks. He said he wanted to stay with Catherine and me. At the last minute, Dick changed his mind. He bolted across the tracks in front of the oncoming train. It didn't miss him by more than a couple of feet. I stood there, frozen, too scared to scream.

By early July, the house was rebuilt and ready to move into. We would be glad to get out of the cramped, upstairs quarters over the Ferdeans. Our whole family--four kids and two adults--had been squeezed into two rooms, living mostly out of tin cans and cardboard boxes.

Dad came in from work one Saturday very downcast. He told Mom that El Ferdean had decided he didn't want us to live in the new house after all. El said he was afraid we'd burn it down again. He fired Dad.

Mom cried and cried. "We don't have any place to live," she groaned.

Webb - #2

Monday, the fifth of July 1937, found us moving back to Webb. Dad rented a place for us to stay and he went back to doing day labor at a dollar a day.

The house he rented was on a farm one-and-a-half miles northeast of town. It was owned by the Chamberlains. Amos and Maude Chamberlain lived on an adjoining farm a half-mile west across the section. The two farms were connected by a long lane that ran along a fence-row between the fields. The Chamberlains were an older couple whose kids were all grown and away from home.

The following Friday, the man from the grocery store in Webb drove down to the house and told Mom she had an urgent telephone call. Her family was trying to reach her.

Mom's face blanched. Instinctively she knew something terrible had happened. She asked the man to drive her to the Chamberlains where she could leave us kids. She rode on into town with him.

A half-hour later Mom was back, crying. Her brother Raymond

had drowned near Salt Lake City. She cried and cried. She bemoaned the fact they were stuck up here in this god-forsaken place and she didn't even have the money to go her own brother's funeral.

After that, some of the spark seemed to go out of Mom's life, and an air of hopelessness set in.

Catherine and I started second grade back in Webb. This time I had to stay with my own grade. The teacher, Miss Painter, lacked the authority to move me out of her class into the third-grade room. However, she did her best to keep me occupied with special reading assignments and math projects. Once she brought in fourth grade pupils to demonstrate how they added and subtracted large numbers. I was able to work the same problems with ease.

One day Dad showed up at home driving a car. Until then, he had been limited in the jobs he could take because they had to be within walking distance. Otherwise he had to find someone with whom he could bum a ride. Now that he had wheels, he took a delivery route for the Sunday Des Moines *Register* to pick up a few extra dollars.

Dad's "new" car was a battered, brown 1926 Chevrolet coupe with a rumble seat. He bought it from an automobile junk-yard dealer for the sum of forty dollars--five dollars down and five dollars a month, no interest. The vehicle's fenders were tattered and rusted. The engine had a miss. Dad said he could overhaul the engine, pound out the fenders and give the car a fresh coat of paint. It would be like new.

A neighbor came over on Sunday and helped Dad get the car's engine running smoothly. They decided to paint the car. Dad didn't like the ugly brown color. He thought blue would be much more spiffy. Two men rounded up a can of blue automotive paint and started on the back right fender, using brushes. It quickly became apparent that at the rate they were using up paint they weren't going to have enough to cover the whole vehicle. Better to thin it, they decided. Lacking automotive paint thinner, they tried gasoline instead.

To their chagrin, they learned a hard lesson. Gasoline used as a paint thinner has undesirable side effects. First of all, the pigment in the paint pulled apart into globules, giving the car a mottled appearance. Second, the paint refused to dry. For weeks afterward, it remained tacky to the touch and rubbed off on clothes.

Catherine and I rode with Dad one Sunday morning on his delivery route. The inside of the car was filled with bundled newspapers, so we rode outside in the rumble seat. A rumble seat is a folding seat in the back of a car in the space normally occupied by the trunk. In nice weather, it's a sporty ride. But this was a frosty November morning. Riding back there soon ceased to be fun. We huddled down as close to the floorboard as we could to keep the wind from blowing on us.

When it came time for the Webb School to put on its annual Christmas pageant, I was again scheduled to sing "God Bless America." Mom decided I needed a new suit for the occasion. Taking a gray flannel suit that had come in one of the boxes of clothes from Indianola, she made me a pair of trousers and a matching coat. She made me a blue necktie. Because her sewing machine had been destroyed in the Greenville fire, she had to stitch the apparel entirely by hand.

As each class waited its turn to perform their part of the program, the teachers had the students go to their regular classrooms and sit in their regular seats. The second-graders were much too excited to sit placidly. Myself among them. I turned around to talk with the boy in the desk behind me. In so doing, I spraddled my legs out on both sides of my own seat. Oops! I shouldn't have done that. The hand-sewn seam on my trousers gave way under the sudden strain. To my horror it ripped all the way up the back.

Mortified, I refused to leave my desk until after everyone else had left the room. I motioned frantically for Catherine to come over. I made her walk as closely behind me as she could so people wouldn't see my fanny flapping.

Mom was both amused and annoyed by my tendency to daydream. One day she sent me down to the mail box to mail a letter. Walking down the long lane toward the road, my mind began to wander. I walked right past the mailbox and down the road. Before I realized where I was I was a half-mile away from the house.

Mom got furious with me over two missing bananas. She insisted I was lying when I said I didn't take them.

Mom accused, "Yes you did! They were here this morning, and you were the only one who could have taken them."

She sent me to bed without any supper. This was the first time that had ever happened to me. I couldn't believe she would actually do it. The worst part was hearing the clatter of dishes as the others ate their meal. When supper was over and Mom was washing dishes, Catherine sneaked upstairs with a slice of bread and a boiled potato. She had filched them from her own plate. That helped assuage the hunger pangs, but not my hurt pride.

Next morning, Mom apologized. It turned out that Dad was the guilty party. When he left for work that morning he stuffed two bananas in his overalls pocket. Mom failed to notice them missing until much later in the day. When Dad finally got home at nine o'clock that night he set the record straight. But I was already asleep.

I don't want your millions, mister,
I don't want your diamond ring.
All I want is the right to live, mister;
Give me back my job again.
I don't want your Rolls-Royce, mister,
I don't want your pleasure yacht.
All I want is food for my babies;
Give me my old job back.
Think me dumb if you wish, mister.
Call me green, or blue, or red.
This one thing I sure know, mister;
My hungry babies must be fed.
--"I Don't Want Your Millions, Mister"-1938

7

Illusions of Normalcy

March 1, 1938, was another moving day. This time, to Everly, Iowa. Dad had found a regular job as hired hand on the Winterboer farm.

George Winterboer was a large, jovial man, tall with a protruding stomach. Striped bibbed overalls were his trademark garb. He wore them everywhere but to church, and he probably would have worn them there too if his wife would let him. To us kids he was known familiarly as "George," but we always referred to his wife, Anna, as "Mrs. Winterboer."

Everly, with a population of seven hundred, was a pretty fair-sized town compared with Webb and Gillett Grove. It was located twenty-one miles west of Spencer, the county seat, and was centered primarily around farming activities. For the Alexander family, this necessitated a move of nearly fifty miles.

Dad no longer owned a car and had no way to move the

household furnishings himself. Two of the Winterboer boys came in a truck to help.

Twenty-two-month-old Shirley, who until then had been very warm and outgoing toward strangers, suddenly became very shy and fearful. When the men came into the house to haul away the furniture, she screamed in terror and ran and hid. Her hiding place was behind a set of wire bedsprings leaning against one wall. In her childlike imagination Shirley felt safe and hidden. When it came time to haul the springs away, Shirley screamed again and ran to hide behind Mom.

The Winterboers were a German family. Indeed, much of the surrounding population was of German descent. George had three brothers and a brother-in-law who farmed in the area. There were a number of other German families as well--mostly related to one another through marriage.

Typically, the adults could speak German but their kids couldn't. That allowed the adults to engage in private conversation, to converse in German without their kids understanding what was being said. By the time kids were grown, most had acquired enough German to use the same tactic on their own children.

The Winterboer farm was located on the west side of the road three miles south of Everly. The house where the Alexanders lived was what Iowans called a "tenant" house; that is to say, it was built specifically for keeping a hired hand on the property. It was situated on the main farmstead about a hundred yards south of the main house, separated by a barbed wire fence and a gate that usually was left open.

The tenant house sat close to the road with a small front yard. It was a trailer-sized, one-story dwelling that ran east-west in its long dimension. The east end of the house, the end nearest the road, was an enclosed porch where Catherine, Dick and I slept. In the middle was a living room that ran the full width of the house, heated only by a wood-burning stove. The west end of the house was split into two rooms. The north room was Mom and Dad's bedroom, barely wide enough to hold a full sized bed and still leave room to walk by. Shirley's baby bed was at the foot of their bed. The south room served as a tiny kitchen, barely large enough to hold a range, cupboard and sink. A back stoop opened off the kitchen. A set of stairs led down to a partial basement-storage room by way of the enclosed front porch. A large vegetable garden stretched both south and west of the house.

Dad's pay was $30 a month, with a gallon of milk a day, half a pig in the spring and a half a cow in the fall.

George and Anna Winterboer had seven children, five living at home. The oldest was Eva, age 26, unmarried, and relegated to the role of being an "old maid." She was sickly and fainted a lot. Besides Eva, there were Hannah, 20, very pretty and newly married; Ray, 19, married and living in Everly; Marvin, age 17; Dorothy, known as "Dodie," age 14; Warner, age 9 and a year older than I; and Esther, age 7, the same age as Catherine.

The Winterboers also owned the farm across the road. Living on it, an eighth of a mile to the north, was their other hired hand, Elmer Smith. Elmer and his wife, Flossie, had two boys. Bobbie, my age, had diabetes and wore thick glasses. Tommy was Dick's age. Their house was a regular-sized farmhouse, much more spacious than ours. Elmer's elderly, nearly blind mother lived with them.

A half-mile to our south and on the east side of the road lived Martin and Annie Roskins. Their three children, two boys and a girl, were all teen-agers and went to school in town.

Warner Winterboer was an inch taller than I and a little on the lanky side. He had brownish hair with an unruly wave that wanted to fall down over his forehead. The thing one noticed about Warner was his perpetual look of grave concern--even his play seemed deliberative. He wore a pinched-face expression.

The first thing one noticed about me was my thick shock of red hair and a mass of orange freckles spattered over my face like so many corn flakes. Barefoot and wearing patched bib overalls, I bore the woebegone appearance of thousands of other raggedy-ass, Depression era kids whose families were victimized by the Dust Bowl.

Warner and I took to each other immediately, as did Esther and

Catherine. Each kid found it nice to have someone their own age and sex to play with.

Esther looked like a typical German fraulein. She was large-boned and square-built, with whitish-blond straight hair bobbed along a sharp line just below her ears, as if someone had put a bowl over her head before cutting her hair. In terms of personality, she was exactly the opposite of Warner. She was fun-loving, easily moved to laughter, and continually thinking up new forms of devilment.

Catherine was chunky and round-faced. She had dishwater-blonde hair cut in a shingle style. Her cherubic smile could win anybody's heart. Always on the go, she never sat still a minute.

The two girls became inseparable. Catherine's birthday was April, Esther's in May. Both were tomboys and preferred being dressed in bib overalls.

Dad had a photograph of himself taken as a small child in which Grandma had dressed him in a girl's outfit and styled his hair in long curls. He said the picture was taken when he was still a little girl. "You're born one way," he said, "but when you get to be a certain age you change."

He was only joking, of course, but Catherine believed him. She and Esther could hardly wait for the change to take place. Every day they'd check to see if they were growing a "weeny." They practiced standing up to pee. It never worked. They just peed down their legs.

The girls practically "lived" in the trees trying to catch squirrels and birds. Or they were Tarzan swinging from branch to branch. I wondered why they didn't fall and break their necks.

That summer they caught pigeons that roosted in the hay loft. At one time or another they must have had a hundred of them. They played with them and kissed them, not knowing how dirty pigeons are and how many diseases they carry. Again, it's a wonder they didn't catch something and die from it.

West of the dwellings was a grove of trees, in which stood an old, discarded cookstove. Catherine and Esther made mud pies there. They used real oats, barley, and eggs until George

Winterboer came across a trail of grain and followed where it went. He found thirty egg shells scattered around. That put a stop to their "really good" mud pies.

One afternoon the girls decided to learn to milk a cow. They had seen the grown-ups do it many times. They were sure it wouldn't be hard to learn. In their children's logic, they reasoned that since they were small children they should start with a small cow, namely, a calf.

Unfortunately for them, Ray Winterboer happened to go out to the barn where he witnessed their efforts. The girls had a bull calf locked in a milking stall, pulling on his testicles. They couldn't figure out why they weren't getting any milk in the pail.

To their acute embarrassment, Ray blabbed the story. In his retelling of it, he added his own embellishments. "The bull didn't seem to mind too much," he said.

Poor Dick didn't have any kids to play with. I was off with Warner much of the time. Catherine and Esther pursued their own adventures. So Dick had to find ways to entertain himself. One of his favorite pastimes--which made no sense to me--was running. He would straddle a broomstick, pretend it was a horse, and run around the yard endlessly, whipping himself on the fanny to make himself go faster.

Shirley, age two-and-a-half, couldn't pronounce her own name. If someone asked Shirley her name, it came out "Tootie Ann All-ee-ander." She became known as "Tootie."

She was also "Little Miss Tag-along." She was a chubby, short-legged little thing who always wanted to tag after Catherine and Esther. Catherine repeatedly begged Mom, "Make Shirley quit tagging after me." But her pleas fell on deaf ears. To complicate matters, Shirley's short legs couldn't keep up with the two older girls. She was forever yelling, "Tatie (Katie), wait for me."

Being "Little Miss Tag-along" nearly cost Shirley her life one day. The two older girls didn't know she was tagging along behind them. They went down the back lane to the horse tank. They stopped to dabble in the water. They leaned way over the tank and made circles in the water with a twig. After a few minutes they tired of that activity and moseyed on.

Shirley came behind and wanted to see what they had looked at in the horse tank. She climbed up onto the rim. When she looked in, she lost her balance and tipped over into the tank head first.

George Winterboer was plowing a field on the other side of the fence and saw the whole thing. He was off that plow and across the fence like a bullet. For a big man, he moved surprisingly fast.

He pulled Shirley out of the tank and pumped on her ribs till she vomited up water. If it hadn't been for him, Shirley would have drowned because Catherine and Esther didn't realize anything was wrong until they heard the commotion.

The schoolhouse was three-quarters of a mile to the north. It was a one-room country school where a single teacher taught all eight grades. The only play equipment was a swing and merry-go-round in the front yard. In the back was a single, four-hole outhouse shared alternately by boys and girls. There was a wonderful birch tree for climbing beside the back fence.

The kids walked to school every day, fair weather and foul, even when it snowed.

When the snow was deep, the big kids walked in front and their feet would sink up to the knees in snow. They left holes that the little kids would try to step in. It wasn't easy for the little ones because the big kids had longer strides. They held hands, each one holding on to the one behind, so if one got stuck they could pull him out. They never lost anyone.

Our teacher for the remainder of that school year was Mrs. Ruby Kiester, a substitute. The regular teacher had moved away earlier in the year. Mrs. Kiester did little more than give the kids reading assignments and maintain order in the classroom. She seldom came outdoors to supervise recess. That period often turned into a rowdy free-for-all.

Coordinating the outhouse activities posed a problem. The girl's outhouse had been destroyed when a tree fell on it a few months earlier and hadn't been rebuilt. So the boys and girls had to take turns using the same facility. Unfortunately, the boys would run out there as soon as recess was announced to get ahead of the girls. They thought it great fun to "hose" the place down. That made it necessary for the girls to straddle the seat rather than sit on it.

I was the new kid in school. One of the older boys decided to initiate me. He took a stick half the length of a broom handle and swizzled it around in the hole of the outhouse until one end was coated with excrement. He carried it behind his back and sidled up to where I was standing. He whipped out the stick and thrust it towards my belly like a sword. Startled, I instinctively grabbed the end of the stick to protect myself. My hands got covered with the smelly stuff.

I silently vowed revenge. My chance came a couple of weeks later. Mrs. Kiester sent me to the cloakroom as punishment for misbehaving in class. While contemplating my fate, my eyes spotted my tormentor's lunch pail. Nobody was watching, so I lifted the lid and peed in it.

The best thing Mrs. Kiester did for Catherine and me was to stress hygiene and personal grooming. She kept a big chart on the wall with all the pupils' names on it. She pasted on little silver stars for having hair combed, teeth brushed, and clothes clean. Our family didn't own a toothbrush. To the best of my recollection I had never brushed my teeth. Since there wasn't money to buy toothbrushes, and we wanted badly to collect the stars, Mom made each of us a toothbrush by wrapping a stick tightly with a piece of cloth. Having no toothpaste, we dipped our "brushes" in salt.

Every morning thereafter, Catherine and I faithfully brushed our teeth to win stars. Our previously brown-stained teeth turned to a gleaming white.

Our vegetable garden was an L-shaped area that ran along the south and west sides of the property. Dad plowed it with a team. Catherine and I helped Mom take full advantage of this large area.

According to Iowa tradition, gardeners have to get their potatoes in the ground by Good Friday. Mom showed us how to cut up potatoes into small pieces with an "eye" in each piece. The eyes were the seed to grow a potato plant. She planted four rows, each about the length of the house.

She also planted two short rows of sweet corn, half a dozen popcorn plants, beets, radishes, carrots, cabbages, onions, leaf lettuce, rutabagas, peas, beans, cucumbers, dill, and tomatoes.

At my insistence, Mom planted some spinach because, as I bragged, "That's what makes Popeye strong."

On the northwest corner she planted asparagus, and on the north fence she planted those funny-looking snow peas.

Mom saw a promotional offer for Beefsteak tomatoes. She sent for them and received 200 tomato plants in the mail. She grew beautiful tomatoes, but she had so many she couldn't even give them away.

Mom introduced sweet potatoes (yams) into northern Iowa. No one around Everly had seen them before. At first people were reluctant to try them, but after Mom showed them how to cook sweet potatoes they liked them fine.

Another thing that grew in great abundance was rhubarb. It grew wild along fence rows like weeds. Mom also grew eggplant which she sliced, breaded, and fried with green tomatoes and onions.

Tending that big a garden required more hands than just Mom's, as Catherine and I found out. Throughout the summer we spent at least two very dull and boring hours every day hoeing and pulling weeds. Dick, now four, turned out to be more bother than help--not because he wasn't willing to try, but because he hadn't learned to tell the difference between weeds and vegetables.

Too poor to afford a radio, phonograph, or other form of entertainment, our family often amused themselves with word games. One night after supper, Mom posed this riddle: "What are the three most important vegetables in the garden?"

I thought and thought. Finally I gave up. I didn't know the answer. Catherine didn't either.

"Lettuce, turnip and pea," Mom said, laughing.

Dick, wanting to be a part of the fun, piped up and said, "I know one, I know one."

Mom turned to him. "Okay, Dick, let's hear your joke."

"What are the three most important parts of a stove?" he asked.

"I don't know," everyone said, going along with the game.

"Lifter, leg and poker," Dick said innocently.

Mom was taken aback. "Where in the world did you hear that?" It was obvious he had no comprehension of its meaning.

"Dad," was his one-word reply. It seemed apparent Dick had picked up the story from one of his Dad's joke-telling sessions, because those were the kinds of raunchy jokes that Dad loved to tell.

At the end of summer, I found weeding and hoeing was only half the work. Canning is a lot harder. As the tomatoes, peas and beans ripened, they had to be put up in jars.

First, the vegetables were picked, sorted, and cleaned. Then they were packed in glass jars and placed in a copper-bottom boiler up to their necks in water with their lids screwed on lightly. The jars were brought to a slow boil and kept there for ten minutes, at which time they were removed and their lids screwed down tightly. As soon as the jars cooled, they were carried down to the cellar and stored.

It was a wonder Mom didn't collapse from heat exhaustion, slaving as she did over a wood-burning stove and steaming kettles during the hottest part of summer. She did it, knowing her efforts would feed her family through the long, cold winter.

"We eat what we can, and what we can't we can," she joked, echoing an old farmwife's motto.

Mom put up more than two hundred jars that year. Still the garden kept yielding produce. She had so many tomatoes she put up a sign on the fence facing the road offering, "Tomatoes Free

For The Picking." Several passersby did stop and take some home with them, but still we ended up feeding several bushels to the hogs.

Dad was mowing hay one day in a swampy area and came across a bunch of frogs. He mentioned he thought he'd catch some and bring them home so we could have frog legs for dinner. Mom hit the ceiling. No way was anyone going to have frog legs in her house.

When Dad went back to the field after lunch he sneaked out with one of Mom's bleached-out flour sacks that she used to make dish towels. He came home with it half-full of frogs, maybe thirty in all. He stashed them in the barn.

Mom went to the main house that evening to ride into town with the Winterboers. After she left, Dad got his sack of frogs. He carried them to an old tree stump to cut off their legs with the blade of his axe.

Mom had forgotten something and came back to the house. She saw Dad with the frog legs. She started screaming. It could have been because of the sight of the frogs themselves or because Dad ruined one of her good bleached flour sacks.

Dad said he'd pay Catherine and me each a nickel if we'd cook them. This was our first experience at cooking frog legs. They twitch while frying, making it look as if they're still alive. We ended up with flour all over the floor, burning lard in the skillet, and frog legs jumping everywhere. It was a terrible mess.

Neither Catherine nor I liked to do dishes; yet that was our regular chore. We continually squabbled over whose turn it was. "I did them last night," one might say, to which the other would reply, "Yes, but I did them for you twice last week?" Mom usually ended up having to referee.

Catherine had a habit of setting aside the used, dirty fruit jars which she hated to wash. She'd hide them 'way back in the corner of the pantry. One night when it was my turn to do the dishes, she started dragging out the food-hardened, moldy fruit jars. There must have been thirty of the gosh-awful things. I let out a squawk. Mom came to investigate and quickly perceived what was going on. She let me go. Catherine, however, spent the entire evening washing fruit jars. Her stunt backfired on her.

When Dick turned five in December 1938, Catherine and I felt he was now old enough to take his turn at doing dishes. We prevailed upon Mom. She agreed.

Dick, however, was not thrilled with the decision. He protested loudly. However, his protests fell on deaf ears. Mom, having made up her mind, was not one to back down.

Dick had a penchant for flailing his arms forcefully when angry. He got so carried away in arguing this matter that he banged one hand against the kitchen stove, burning it badly. As a result, he put himself out of commission for doing the dishes that night--or for several nights thereafter.

Catherine accused him of having burned his hand on purpose to get out of doing dishes.

Dick would eat almost anything that was set in front of him. Catherine and I put this theory to the test one Saturday night when we were dawdling at the table after supper. Dad had gone into town to buy the weekly groceries, and Mom was in the outhouse attending to nature's call. We had finished our dessert of boiled prunes and were playing around with the pits.

I bet Dick he couldn't swallow one. He said he could. I offered to pay him a penny for every prune pit he could swallow. He accepted the offer. Catherine and I egged him on as he swallowed one after another. He had downed eleven pits by the time Mom came back in the house and discovered what we were up to.

She became hysterical. "That's a stupid goddamn thing to do," she railed at me and Catherine. Poor Dick was scared half to death. He got down off his chair and cowered in the corner.

"What in the hell did you kids think you were doing?" she demanded. She said Dick might get an intestinal blockage and the pits would have to be removed by surgery.

Catherine was remorseful at first. She didn't want anything bad to happen to her little brother. But soon her impish nature took over and she began to tease him. "Those prune seeds will make a tree grow out of your belly. A bird will come sit in the tree and poop in your face," she said.

Dick, conjuring up images of all sorts of horrible things happening to him, puckered up his lips and began to cry. "Mom, is a tree going to grow out of my belly?" he asked plaintively.

Mom sought to reassure him. "Of course not," she said, ordering Catherine to stop saying that.

Catherine didn't give up easily. When Mom wasn't looking, she would whisper loud enough for Dick to hear, "Dick's going to have a tree grow out of his belly."

Dick let out a louder wail.

Mom swatted Catherine on the behind and sent her to the kitchen. Soon we heard another unhappy wail. This time, it came from Catherine. Although tonight would have been Dick's turn to wash dishes, Mom released him from that onerous duty and said we two older kids would have to do them instead. Catherine did not accept her punishment gracefully. She grumbled all the while she was washing. I dried in silence, worried that I might have caused Dick irreparable harm.

As for Dick, he reveled in his image of indestructibility. Two days later he passed the pits without incident.

Warner and I made ourselves useful during the threshing season, and we earned spending money to boot.

Threshing was the most intensive work of the year. When the oats and barley ripened in late July, the farmer harvested them with a horse-drawn machine called a "grain binder." This ungainly contraption had mower blades that ran across the front to cut the stalks off near the ground. Big, rotating egg-beater paddles swept the grain-laden stalks backward onto a moving canvas platform. The moving platform carried the grain into a hopper where it was tied in bundles about twelve inches thick and deposited on the ground behind the binder as it moved along.

The bundles--"sheaves" as they were called in the Bible--had to be stacked upright in shocks for drying. If allowed to lay on the ground their heads would rot. To make a shock of grain, the field hand grabbed two bundles and stood them up against each other. Then he circled them with six more upright bundles. Finally, he took another bundle and laid it across the top for a cap.

After a week or more of standing in shocks, it was time for the threshing activities. This was a massive operation involving numerous men and expensive machinery. For the sake of economy most farmers banded together in a kind of communal activity, five or six to a circuit, called a "round." They took turns working each farm until all were done.

The threshing operation took place in two arenas. One was in the fields where men with horse-drawn hayracks loaded the shocked grain for hauling into the threshing machine. Customarily, there were two men on the ground wielding pitchforks who pitched the bundles up onto the hayrack, while the man on top arranged them into a stable load. Two such crews worked at all times.

The second arena was the threshing operation itself back at the farmyard. The threshing machine was a huge monster that drew its power from a pulley and belt connected to the tractor. One end of the machine was dominated by an elevated conveyer belt about ten feet long.

The conveyer was double-sided so as to handle two hayracks at a time, one on each side. The drivers would pull up alongside and pitch off the bundles of grain into the trough. The bundles were carried into a set of terrible-looking, whirling blades. They were gobbled up by this hungry maw where they disappeared into the dark and mysterious interior of the machine, soon to emerge from the other end in two streams--one of straw and the other of golden grain.

Lots of gruesome stories were told about men who fell into a threshing machine and were chopped to pieces. I think that's all they were, stories, for I never met anyone who actually witnessed that fate.

Warner and I shared the job of shoveling grain around the wagon as it flowed out the machine's nozzle. This was necessary to even the load so it wouldn't pile up in the middle and spill over the sides. As soon as one wagon was full, a worker would drive it off to unload at the granary. Another took its place.

Although our work wasn't particularly hard it was hot and dusty. It gave us a sense of responsibility. Each was paid fifty cents a week. Even more rewarding than the money, however, was the fact we were accorded the same treatment as the men and got to sit at the main table with them at dinner.

Iowa threshing dinners were legendary. The womenfolk, like the men, engaged in a kind of communal effort. They prepared prodigious amounts of food. Some worked in the host kitchen. Others sent pies or cakes with their menfolk.

Some of the farmers came early enough for breakfast. Mrs. Winterboer stood at the stove making dishpans full of donuts. Catherine and Esther got to put them in the sack and shake sugar on them.

At mid-morning, women would go out to the field with tubs of sandwiches, cookies and lemonade or coffee to feed the men. This was called "lunch."

Threshing operations shut down for the noon hour and the men came in from the fields. They stopped at either the horse tank or washstand to slop water over themselves to rinse off the caked layers of dust. Still dripping wet from sweat and water, they crowded around a huge table laden with steaming platters of roast beef, fried chicken, mashed potatoes, milk gravy, fresh-baked bread, and several kinds of cooked vegetables. They stoked away enormous quantities. I found it difficult to eat because somebody was always asking for this or that platter to be passed. Then about the time I felt I couldn't possibly stuff down another bite, the women came in with gigantic slabs of apple, cherry or raisin pie.

At mid-afternoon, more sandwiches were brought out to workers the field. Some men stayed for supper, too.

By tradition, the last farm on the threshing round would furnish a party the last day. That year, it was Conn Winterboer, George's brother. When the last wagon was unloaded and the last piece of machinery shut down, Conn wheeled out washtubs filled with fermented cider and chilled bottles of Grainbelt beer. With harvest done, it was time for the celebrating to begin.

This being a German community, no one was shy about guzzling beer. Nor did anyone seem to mind that Warner and I helped ourselves to a bottle, then another, and another.

I drank two-and-a-half bottles before my belly got full and I couldn't swallow any more. Perhaps it was the hot weather, or the beer, but I began having trouble getting from one place to another. When I tried to take the harness off the horse, I walked into its side. I backed off and made another run at it, but no matter how hard I tried, I couldn't get where I was aiming. Worse, I couldn't understand why all the men were laughing at me, Dad included.

Finally, George took me by the arm and led me over under a shade tree. He sat me down. "No more beer for you, son," he said firmly.

George Winterboer journeyed to Sioux City at the end of summer to sell cattle. He came back in a new Lincoln Zephyr. Paid $600 for it. Everybody came to look.

He also brought back a watermelon so big it would barely fit in a galvanized wash tub. He iced it down all day, and that night we had a watermelon party. The grownups sat out in the yard and told jokes while the kids played games.

Ray Winterboer began teasing me about my freckles. A couple of other folk chimed in. I guess I looked pretty down in the mouth because Cora, Ray's young bride, came to my aid. She said, "That's all right, James. Kids with freckles are all really smart."

With those words of encouragement, I smiled from ear to ear.

The party was enlivened by the Winterboers' three-legged dog named Buzzy. He'd lost one leg in a mowing accident. Right in the middle of festivities, Buzzy and a she-dog decided to get "married." We kids tried to break up the romance by throwing cold water on the lovers. The grownups snickered, saying, "Let them go." Catherine thought the dogs were in great pain because they made so much noise. After ten minutes or so of moaning and groaning, the dogs separated and we kids went back to playing our game of "Kick the Can."

The Clay County Fair, held at Spencer, carried a reputation as being the largest fair in northwest Iowa. Some said it rivaled the Iowa State Fair at Des Moines.

Our family rode to the fair with Harley Teeters and his family, for a total of ten people piled atop of one another in a single car. The Teeters lived on a rent-farm two miles west and were about as poor as the Alexander family. On the way, Dad handed Mom a pad of blank counter checks and had her write out two checks, one to him and one to Harley. Mom protested, saying she was "scared." But Dad insisted. He told her what amounts to write in and what names to sign on them.

The car stopped at a grocery store while Dad went in. He got cash and a couple of dollars worth of groceries with the check. He didn't encounter any difficulty in cashing the check. We stopped at another grocery store and Harley did the same thing. From the proceeds, they gave each child fifty cents to spend at the fair.

We kids had to get all our rides in before five o'clock while the price was still a nickel. After five, the fares went up to a dime.

We ran into the Ferdean family from Greenville who were also attending the fair. The three families got together for a picnic supper on a grassy knoll near where the cars were parked. From that vantage point we watched the free fireworks display.

Catherine and I began the third grade that September with a new teacher. She was also new to the teaching profession. Miss Mary Meyers was eighteen years old and had finished one year of teachers college. She lived just a few miles to the east.

Miss Meyers was nice-looking, medium height and build, with dark hair cut fairly short. She radiated both sincerity and warmth. She wore octagonal-framed glasses--a style I had never seen before.

She was in charge of a school with students spread across eight grades. She rose to the occasion. She put an end to the boys' foolishness at the outhouse. She made sure the girls went first. She supervised recess and put an end to rowdiness and fighting.

The lone eighth-grader was a girl named Mary Dykstra. She was large and ungainly, wore wire-rimmed glasses and had stringy hair. She generally kept to herself--definitely not a popular girl. One day Miss Meyers had the primary group up front, reading a story. It was about some little lambs that got lost. "They went, maa, maa, maa," she read aloud.

From the back of the room came a loud, booming voice. "Yeah, and the big buck went BAA, BAA, BAA." Everyone turned to look. It was Mary Dykstra.

A short time later, Mary stopped coming to school. She never finished the eighth grade.

Miss Meyers managed to acquire several pairs of clamp-on, steel-wheeled roller skates. She persuaded some of the parents to help clean out the basement so the kids could skate there during the winter months. The smooth concrete floor made a nice skating rink. The boys found delight in chasing around behind the furnace where they had to duck under pipes.

The only time I saw Miss Meyers get flustered was one wintry morning when we kids showed up at school and found her standing outside. She had gone to the basement to light the furnace and found a skunk there. Warner and I ventured down to take a look. Sure enough, there was a small female skunk cowering near the furnace. Evidently, she had come inside to get away from the cold. She was probably as scared as we were. When Warner and I ventured too close, she arched her back and hissed at us.

We went back outside to confer. Everyone else was huddling in the cold. Miss Meyers had sent one of the pupils to fetch Warner's dad.

Warner was not inclined to wait. He said, "If we pick up a skunk by its tail, its legs can't get enough traction to squirt you." He proposed that I be the one to distract the skunk's attention while he sneaked sneak up behind her and grabbed her tail.

We went back down into the basement and put his plan to work. It worked beautifully. By the time old man Winterboer got there, the crisis was over. Warner had already carried the frightened and struggling skunk to a nearby field and turned her loose. (Note: When I visited Miss Meyers in 1995, more than 50 years later, her first question to me was, "Do you remember the time we had the skunk in the basement?")

Miss Meyers had a lot of programs on holidays and the last day of school. All the parents came.

For Thanksgiving, she arranged for the schoolchildren to put on a pageant for their parents. It was on Wednesday afternoon so the kids could go on home with their families when it was over. One role called for a three-year-old child to come on stage and utter one line. It had to be done just right because it was the "curtain line" that ended the play.

Miss Meyers asked Catherine and me if we thought Shirley could do it. We asked our Mom, and she convinced Shirley to say she would. On the big day, everything came off to perfection. The closing scene had all the kids, dressed in Pilgrims' costumes, say what they were going to bring to Thanksgiving. They said they'd bring corn, peas, pheasants and pies. At the very end they asked, "What about Baby Dumpling? What is she going to bring?"

That was Shirley's cue. She toddled onstage wearing a bunny costume and delivered her one big line: "I bring an appetite!"

The Saturday before Christmas, the Teeters came by and everyone piled in their car to go shopping in Spencer. On the way, Dad cashed a couple more bad checks.

The city of Spencer was decked out for Christmas. The main street had been turned into an open-air shopping mall. The kids lined up to go through the Santa Claus sleigh parked in the middle of the street. Each received a peppermint candy cane. Then the families split up and went their separate ways with the understanding everyone would meet back at the same place at three o'clock.

I had a whole dollar to spend. I browsed through the stores looking for things cheap enough that I could buy gifts for everyone. I paid a nickel for a plastic flower that Mom could pin to her lapel. For Dad, I bought a pair of boot-laces. In Woolworth's Five and Ten, I saw a large, blonde, Shirley Temple doll that I wanted to buy for Catherine. There was no way I could come up with the required $2.98. So I contented myself with buying her a diary for twenty-five cents that had a brass lock on it. That was my biggest purchase of the day.

At the toy counter, I fell in love with an ivory-handled, cowboy six-shooter with a studded holster and cartridge belt. My heart ached to own it. Several times I returned to the counter to take the gun lovingly out of the holster and imagine I was fighting a band of outlaws.

Temptation finally got the best of me. Looking around to be sure no clerks were near, I slipped the gun under my coat and sidled out the door.

I didn't show the gun to anyone until after we got home. Mom threw a hissy fit. She refused to believe my story when I tried to convince her I found it laying on the sidewalk. I said, "Somebody probably dropped it." She insisted I was lying, took the gun away, and said I was going to have to take it back where I got it.

The next morning in church, I prayed for God to forgive me. I resolved never to steal again. Stealing was just too darn much trouble.

That was the Christmas when I learned for sure there was no Santa Claus. I'd been told that many times before, but I never wanted to believe it. The revelation came when Dad went to the basement to get presents. His path took him by the bed where Catherine and I slept. Only, I wasn't asleep. I only pretended to be. By lying still and peeking through a slender crack in my eyelids, I was able to watch Dad place the presents under the tree. The next morning I saw that all of the presents brought by "Santa" were exactly the same presents Dad and Mom bought in Spencer the previous Saturday.

Even though I now realized there was no Santa, I didn't say anything to Catherine and Dick. I didn't want to ruin their fun.

The Saturday after Christmas, the Winterboer boys were going to Spencer. Mom asked them if they would take me along. She said I had something important to do. That "something important" was to take the purloined gun back into Woolworths.

The empty holster was no longer on the counter. So I laid the gun on the counter and slipped out without saying anything. I was glad to get that ordeal over!

Arguments between Mom and Dad became more frequent as the winter wore on and through the following spring. Their extreme poverty weighed heavily on Mom. She just didn't see any way out of it. She accused Dad of being spineless. She said he talked a good line but lacked the will to amount to anything. She begged him to move to town and get a decent paying job so they could live a "normal life." Dad was unwilling to let go of farming--the only way of life he understood.

At the end of canning season, Mom decided to take matters into her own hands. If Dad was too spineless to get off the farm, she was going to do it for him. She packed a suitcase and took a Greyhound bus to Sioux Falls, South Dakota, about ninety miles to the west. She stayed with some distant cousins, Betty and "Webb" Webster. She took a job as a waitress in a restaurant to save up money for moving expenses. She spent her nonworking hours trying to line up a job Dad could handle.

Catherine and I were saddled with the duties of taking care of the household while Mom was away. Marie Roskins from down the road helped out. We cooked meals, washed dishes, and looked after Dick and Shirley. Our diet consisted mostly of boiled potatoes, canned vegetables, cornbread, cabbage salad, and occasionally meat whenever we could afford it. For breakfast Dad had to have his fried potatoes while the kids ate their usual regimen of oatmeal. The fare was pretty plain, but we managed to get by.

When school started again in the fall I began the fifth grade. Miss Meyers had finally persuaded Mom and Dad to let me skip a grade. For the first time, Catherine and I were not in the same class, although this being a one-room school, we were still in the same room.

Dick started school in the primary grade. He talked with a lisp and Miss Meyers had trouble understanding him. Catherine and I often had to translate.

Mrs. Winterboer took care of Shirley during school hours.

Then Dad got put in jail. The sheriff's deputies came out and got him one day and hauled him off to Spencer. He, along with his buddy, Harley Teeters, was charged with writing bad checks. Dad had cashed quite a few bad checks during the past year, all for piddling amounts.

It was now up to me and Catherine, ages nine and eight, respectively, to hold the family together during the absence of both parents. We carried on as before.

A social worker came to check out the situation. She was aghast to discover four children living alone together without an adult in the house. She persuaded the court to let Dad out on probation so he could get back and take care of his children. She also got in contact with Mom--who until then hadn't known Dad was in jail. She warned her if she didn't come back home immediately, the county was going to take her kids away and put them in foster homes.

The twenty-sixth of September found a remorseful Mom back home again.

George Winterboer informed Dad that he could work through the winter, but he was not going to renew his contract come spring. He said it was his practice to change hired hands every two years. The Alexander family would have to move again.

That was devastating news to us kids. We had begun to think of ourselves as part of the Winterboers' extended family.

These two years were the most normal times I had ever known.

Raggedy, raggedy are we,
Just as raggedy as raggedy can be,
We don't get nothing for our labor,
So raggedy, raggedy are we.
So hungry, hungry are we,
Just as hungry, as hungry can be,
We don't get nothing for our labor,
So hungry, hungry are we.
--Tune: "How Beautiful Heaven Would Be"
--Words: John Handcox

8

Bare Feet and Bib Overalls

March 1, 1940, was moving day. I had just passed my tenth birthday. It was hard saying goodbye to Warner and Esther Winterboer, who had become like brother and sister to Catherine and me.

We packed our belongings in a rented truck and headed for the town of Lake Park, which was located near the Minnesota border about twenty-five miles north of Everly. Some might say we were "moving up" in the world in the sense that Lake Park was a larger town. Its population was half again the size of Everly.

Dad's new job was on a tenant farm two-and-three-quarters miles north of town. The farm was owned by Dr. Wilfred Marks, the town's sole veterinarian. Dad's pay was standard for a hired hand--$30 a month for March through October, $25 a month through the winter. Also, he received a gallon of milk a day, a half a pig in the spring, and a half a beef in the fall.

Our house was situated on the east side of a gravel road, half-way up a rolling hill that topped out at the section line. The Minnesota border was just one mile farther north.

"Doc" Marks and his family lived on a farm a half-mile to the south. His wife's name was Emma. They had 26-year-old twin sons, Wilfred, Jr. ("Bill") and Warren. Bill was a veterinarian in Estherville, and Warren, who had flunked out of vet school, lived at home and worked for his dad.

Doc Marks had another hired hand living on the home place with the unlikely name of Roland Stone. Roland was single and drove a brown 1928 Chevy coupe.

Between the Marks's and us lived the Namany family. They had five kids, all boys, the youngest being Catherine's age. The Namanys were an odd clan who stayed to themselves and didn't socialize much.

Across the section line to the north lived the Rausches. They had one son, Harold, who was my age. Mr. Rausch's mother lived with them.

We kids were happy to have a real house to live in. It was much larger than the tenant house at Everly. The ground floor had a large kitchen-dining room running the full width of the house, a very large living room across the middle, and two full bedrooms.

Upstairs were two sleeping areas plus a smaller, unfinished storage room. The big room at the top of the stairs was for Catherine and Shirley. The smaller room was for Dick and me. To get to our sleeping quarters, Dick and I had to walk through the girls' room.

In the process of moving in, I noticed a brownish-yellow sticky substance seeping down the top of the door jamb between the two bedrooms. I called it to Mom's attention. She, in turn, asked Roland who was helping move furniture. He explained, "Oh, there's a swarm of bees in the side of the house, and that's some of the honey dripping down from the hive."

I went outside to check. Sure enough, there was a bunch of bees flying in and out of a crack in the east side of the house near the roof-line. The thought occurred to me that I might "zap" the bees. I took a softball and began throwing it against the side of the house near the hole where the bees were flying in and out. With each throw, I'd smash a half-dozen or more bees. I kept that up a few minutes, making good progress in reducing the bee population.

The bees soon figured out where the deadly missile was coming from. With military-like precision they joined up in formation and zeroed in on me. They stung me on the face, neck, hands, and anywhere else naked skin was exposed. Swatting furiously, I beat a hasty retreat.

Roland then explained further, "I don't know if Doc Marks told your dad, but this is actually two smaller houses joined together to make one big house. Those bees have taken up residence in the crack between the two houses where they didn't quite fit together."

I went back outside to check--making sure to keep a healthy distance from the bees. Sure enough, a seam ran right through the house along the east-west dimension where the houses were joined. That accounted for the honey dripping down inside. It also explained the arrangement upstairs whereby we boys had to go through the girls' room to get to our own bedroom.

A few weeks after moving in, Mom noticed a funny-looking yellow stain beneath the boys' bedroom window. She couldn't figure out what was causing it. One day, however, she saw water dripping and went to check it out. It turned out to be urine.

The stain was the result of laziness on the part of Dick and me. We felt that the outhouse was too far to walk at night--through the girls' room, down the stairs, and fifty feet down the path, etc. So we were simply hanging our weenies out the window. It worked OK for me, but Dick was much shorter and could barely get his thing over the window sill. His pee dribbled down the wallpaper.

Mom put a stop to that.

Doc Marks had recently built a brand-new, modernistic design barn on the property. *Cappers Weekly*, a farm magazine, ran a picture story on it. The unique feature was an arched roof made with laminated beams, rather than the hipped roof commonly used on barns until that time. It was considered to be trend-setting.

Marks was so proud of his new barn that he had it wired for

Marks was so proud of his new barn that he had it wired for electricity, even though the hired hand's house was not. He said the hired hand's family would run up the electric bill.

Mom owned an electric iron she had acquired at an auction. Since she couldn't use it in the house, she took her ironing out to the barn. One of us kids was always posted to be a lookout in case Doc Marks happened by.

Between the house and the barn were a tool shed and a machinery shed. A windmill and stock tank were just off the corner of the machinery shed near the barn. The windmill was equipped with a one-cylinder Fairbanks-Morse engine as a back-up device to drive the pump when the wind failed. We called this engine a "pop-n-jenny" because of the distinctive sound it made when running.

On the far side of the barn, forming the north side of the barnyard, stood an open-faced cow shed. Two round, galvanized grain bins completed the layout on the south side of the yard.

The outhouse was a "three-holer"--two big holes for adults and one little one for tots. It was situated a few yards off the northeast corner of the house.

A big grove of trees on the north side of the property afforded partial protection from winter's icy winds.

We went to school in Lake Park. A bus picked us up and brought us home.

The school building was a U-shaped, dark brick structure. Elementary grades 1 through 5 occupied both lower-level wings, with the school auditorium in the middle section. Junior high (grades 6-7-8) was on the second-floor west wing, and the high school (grades 9-12) occupied a similar space in the east wing.

My fifth-grade teacher was Miss Schenk, whose name I learned later means "bartender" in German. Unfortunately, that's not the way boys in her class viewed it. They had a mischievous proclivity to pronounce it as "Miss Skunk."

My assigned seat was near the back of the room at a desk formerly occupied by LeRoy Fisher. How did I know? LeRoy left a memorial to his presence by carving his name in the desk top.

Mom was six months pregnant with her fifth child at the time we moved from Everly. She said it happened the week she got back from Sioux Falls. She was so embarrassed about being pregnant again--remarks about "all those kids"--that she never told anyone. Not even her immediate family in Indianola.

She was having a difficult pregnancy. During the final weeks she hired a woman to keep house, Olga Snyder. Olga was in her early fifties. Her most distinguishing feature was a set of false teeth that didn't fit right. They were always going clickety-clack when she talked. And she talked all the time.

Mom's doctor was Dr. Bullock. He lived next door to the school. Sometimes when she was having a bad day, Mom would send notes to school with Catherine to deliver to Dr. Bullock.

Shortly after noon on Wednesday, June 26th, Mom called me into her bedroom. She handed me a note. "Run down the road as fast as you can and deliver this to Mrs. Marks," she instructed. I could see that she was in a great deal of pain.

Mrs. Marks opened the note, read its contents, and immediately got on the telephone to Dr. Bullock. Then she packed towels and some things in a household bucket and drove down to our house. I rode along.

Dr. Bullock got there within twenty minutes. He went into the bedroom to see Mom. When he came out he spoke very briefly with Olga Snyder.

Mom asked for me. I went into the bedroom where she was covered with a sheet. She looked very pale. In a weak voice she said, "I want you to take the kids down to the Marks's. Then I want you to come back and stay here in case I need you. You're the only one I've got."

I walked my brother and sisters to the Marks's as told. Mrs. Marks said she'd look after them. What I didn't realize was that Catherine sneaked away without Mrs. Marks knowing. She hung around the bushes beside our house trying to see what was going on inside.

I wondered why Dad wasn't here at this critical time. He was working out in a field not very far away, yet Mom didn't asked anyone to take word to him. Somehow, I sensed Mom didn't want Dad around. Ultimately, I decided that what was going on between them was none of my business.

After a while of aimlessly trying to find something to do, I got out his stilts and walked around the yard. I "accidentally" passed by Mom's bedroom window a couple of times and glanced in to see what was going on. All I could see was a sheet made into a tent at the foot of the bed. Dr. Bullock's arms reached up under it.

At one point, I witnessed Olga Snyder come out of the house with a bucket, go around back, dig a hole and bury something. It was the afterbirth.

Eventually, Dr. Bullock called me into the house. He said, "Your mother has just had a baby boy. She's very weak now, but she wants to talk to you."

I walked timidly into the bedroom. Mom was lying on the bed with a baby cuddled in her arms. She appeared pale and wan. She smiled weakly. "Say hello to your new baby brother," she said.

I stood near the foot of the bed, not sure what to do.

"I need your help in giving him a name," Mom said.

"Don't you and Dad have a name picked out?" I asked.

"Your Dad wants to name him Jerry. I don't want to name him Jerry. I think it's up to you and me to decide on a name."

I said I'd try. "How about David?" I asked hopefully.

Mom said, "Oh, that's a pretty name. Let's call him David." She paused, then said, "What shall we use for a middle name?"

After trying several names for sound, we came up with the name Dean. I'm not sure who thought of it first.

She liked it. "That has a nice sound to it--David Dean. That's what we'll name him, David Dean."

Those were the names Mom gave the doctor to write on the birth certificate: David Dean Alexander, Lake Park, Iowa, June 26, 1940.

Mom cautioned me, "Your Dad's going to be madder than hell when he finds out we didn't name him Jerry. Just let him get mad. Serves him right."

Dr. Bullock, before he left, told me that my mother nearly bled to death having the baby. At one point he wasn't sure he could save her. She was going to have to stay in bed for at least the next ten days. He suggested we get her a covered bucket because he didn't want her using the outhouse. If she started bleeding again, call him immediately. He handed Mrs. Snyder a bucket full of blood-soaked sheets and towels.

As it turned out, Mom was right about Dad's anger. He didn't get as mad about the name David Dean as he did because she didn't tell him she went into labor.

"It's a helluva goddamn note to come in from work and find your wife has delivered a baby," he ranted. "She didn't even have the courtesy to tell me about it. Everybody on God's green earth knew about it before me!"

A couple of days later while Mom was still confined to bed, four-year-old Shirley brought her a surprise. It was bowl of mulberries she had picked by herself. They were full of twigs, leaves, and dirt as well as cream and sugar. Shirley was pleased with herself and her surprise. The other kids had a laugh. Mom ate them like a good sport.

The census-taker came around to take the 1940 census. After he finished his interview, the man told Mom, "You're the first family I've ever interviewed that doesn't own a radio."

Mom told that story to Dad when he came home for supper. She said it so sarcastically there was no doubt she didn't mean it to be funny.

Shirley was a sensitive little girl who felt things more keenly than the others. Mom put her to work shelling green peas from the garden. What started out as a fun chore soon lost its luster. She whined to stop. Mom, whose nerves and patience were worn thin, was not sympathetic to this little worker, and said crossly, "If you don't work, you don't eat!" Shirley continued on with the dreadful job, but her sensitive little heart was broken by the harsh words. Reality of life came at an early age to Depression kids.

One day Shirley was playing among the trees that shaded the north side of the house when she spied a sheep lying on the ground. Her curiosity led her to examine it. The animal was dead. As she got closer, she saw it was being eaten by maggots. She was shocked and repulsed. Later, the other kids teased her by singing a gruesome ditty, "Oh, the worms crawl in, the worms crawl out. The worms play pinochle on your snout."

It was standard practice for the girls to get their hair washed on Saturday afternoons. Mom would fetch the tin wash pan and fill it with boiling water from the teakettle. She'd add enough cold water to make it the right temperature. The problem was, what seemed like the "right" temperature for her work-hardened hands was not always the right temperature for sensitive scalps.

Then the scrubbing would begin. One day as her mother scrubbed, Shirley looked down into the water. She was amazed to see how much dirt had come out of her hair.

Rinsing was another torture. With the girls' heads all warm and soapy, Mom sent them into "shock" by pouring cold well water over their heads. They gasped and yelled. Mom added vinegar to the rinse water to cut the soap residue and to keep Shirley's blonde hair bright and shiny.

I launched my radio career at an early age. My radio station was comprised of a wooden cigar box with a make-believe microphone on it. Across the front of the box I painted the call letters, S H I T. I practiced broadcasting every day until Mom put a stop to it. She didn't think my call letters were very funny.

One morning Catherine and I set out to go fishing. We dug worms and put them in a jar. Inadvertently we left the jar behind. Not until we'd walked the two miles to the lake did we discover we didn't have any worms.

We probed around in some garbage cans and found a few orange peels. We reasoned that fish were dumb and may not notice the difference.

Apparently, fish aren't as dumb as we thought. They sure knew the difference between juicy worms and sour orange peels.

Consequently, Catherine and I didn't catch a single fish. But we did have a good time.

Dick was a bed wetter. Every night, just before going to bed himself, Dad walked Dick out to the outhouse. Dick was generally so sleepy his eyes would be closed and Dad would have to guide him along the way. Still Dick wet the bed.

Dr. Bullock said the reason for it was that Dick always moved at a dead run. By the time he went to bed he "died." That is, he lacked the energy to wake himself the way most people do.

The outhouse was the one place members of the household could be guaranteed privacy. It was furnished with a Sears and Roebuck catalog--known as a "wish-and-wonder" book. Its pages served the practical function of toilet paper. It was also reading matter. By the time the occupants worked their way back to the leather goods pages, it was about time for the new catalog to come in the mail.

Catherine saved the wrapping papers from a couple of lugs of peaches Mom bought. She smoothed them out and had nice soft toilet paper for a while. It sure beat the Sears catalog.

As a little joke, Dad put three corncobs on the outhouse wall. He said, "First you use one of the red cobs. Then you use the white cob to see if you need the other red one."

Numerous clumps of rhubarb grew wild along the fence. Mom canned rhubarb, made rhubarb pie, and served rhubarb pudding for dessert. Still, there was more rhubarb there than we could ever eat.

Often we kids would get a cup of sugar, break off a stalk of rhubarb, dip it in sugar, and chew out the juices. We spit out the pulp. Raw rhubarb was so tart it set our teeth on edge.

Dad got the bright idea one time of making rhubarb wine. He and a man named Foster, whom I scarcely knew, gathered up all the rhubarb stalks they could find, ran them through the clothes-wringer of Mom's washing machine, and caught the juice in her laundry tub. Mom wasn't too happy about that.

Dad and his pal mixed in sugar, yeast, raisins, and whatever other ingredients they thought was needed, and poured the concoction into five-gallon buckets. They covered the buckets with cloth and stored them upstairs in the catch-all room to ferment. Every day Dad went upstairs to check the progress of fermentation. The fumes grew to be so strong that sometimes it made us kids dizzy just sleeping up there.

Finally, the day came when Dad and Foster solemnly pronounced that the wine had fermented long enough. They bottled it in quart fruit jars, screwed the caps on tight, and stored them in the basement under the house.

Unfortunately, the wine was still green. Or maybe it had too much yeast in it. In any event, it had not stopped fermenting. The internal pressure built up so strong inside the jars that every once in a while one of them would explode.

All the rest of the summer, we often heard a "BOOM" beneath our feet. Someone would say, "There goes another jar of rhubarb wine."

Dad did his manful best to drink as many bottles as he could before they exploded. Forty quarts was a lot of wine for one man to drink.

Dick started the primary grade all over again. Mom felt he hadn't learned much in the one-room school at Everly.

Mom put Dick on the bus with Catherine and me, and told us to see he got enrolled. We led him as far as the classroom door, then sent him inside.

Six weeks later, Dick came home with his first report card. The name on the report card read "John Alexander." Mom asked why.

Dick explained matter-of-factly. "Well, when they went around the room asking names, somebody else already had the name Richard. So I took John."

Dick had an independent streak. "Bull headedness," Dad called it. For example, the school set up a deal whereby all the kids would get their vaccination shots *en masse*. It was arranged so that after school they would board buses as usual and go to the clinic for shots before going home. Dick was not keen on the idea of getting stuck with a needle. Instead of boarding the bus he simply walked off the school grounds and headed home.

When the bus dropped Catherine and me off at our house, Dick was not with us. Mom asked, "Where's Dick?"

We looked at each other and shrugged, "We thought he was on the bus with us."

Mom was frantic. But she needn't have worried. Fifteen or twenty minutes later, here came Dick trudging down the road, totally unconcerned. He'd walked the whole two-and-three-quarters miles by himself.

To say that Dick was bull headed was more than a figure of speech. He sometimes acted like a bull.

I had a male guernsey calf which I had been raising. It was kept tied up behind the house. Ordinarily, Doc Marks knocked the male dairy calves in the head at birth because they couldn't give milk, and they were too expensive to raise for beef. But Dad talked Marks into letting me have one of the calves he otherwise would have killed.

Our deal was Dad would provide the feed, I the labor, and we would split the proceeds. Dad considered it good discipline. Morning and night, good weather and bad, I saw to it that the calf got fed and watered.

That calf nearly proved to be Dick's undoing, however. Dick liked to pretend he was a bull and butt heads with the calf. Sometimes he butted the calf so hard that it was the calf, not Dick, who reeled backwards.

One evening when the calf was about three months old, I was watching as Dick and the calf butted heads. After one of those butts Dick began wandering around the yard in circles, completely dazed. Unbeknownst to him, the calf had begun to sprout horns. They were only the size of a man's knuckle, but one of them drilled Dick dead center. That episode cured Dick of that sport.

Doc Marks was a prudish person. Even though he castrated pigs, delivered calves, etc., he didn't enjoy jokes about such things when it came to people.

He was at the farm one day supervising activities. Dick was trailing him around. Dick had to wee-wee. He flipped out his thing and went beside the wagon. He hollered up at Marks, "Hey Doc, I need a new weenie. This one's got a leak in it."

Dad laughed uproariously, but Doc turned red in the face.

Armistice Day, November 11, blew in the most devastating blizzard in northern Iowa's history. It came without warning. But Dad had a premonition.

The day before, he ordered us kids to go out and bring the cattle into the barn. It was a bright, sunshiny day, and we procrastinated. Dad fussed at us. We brought the cattle in just before dark.

The blizzard swept in overnight. Fifty-mile-an-hour gale winds and snowfall up to twelve inches clogged highways and shut down communications. An airplane lost its way and plunged into Spirit Lake, fifteen miles east. Drifts piled ten and twelve feet high. Scores of hunters were trapped in duck blinds on lakes and rivers as the cold swept in. At least twenty-six were known to have died.

During a let-up in the storm, Dad made his way out to the barn to get some rope. He lashed one end to the barn door and tied the other around his waist. He groped his way out to the cattle shed, secure in the knowledge that if he lost his way in the blinding snow he could 'reel' himself back to the barn.

Later, he tried the same tactic for getting back to the house. The rope wasn't long enough and he came to its end before the house came into view. Drifts were waist-high and he couldn't be sure where he was, or where the house was. He realized it could be fatal to strike off in the wrong direction.

He made his way back as far as the machinery shed where he provisioned himself with an armload of wood. Then he struck off towards the house again. When he reached the end of his rope this second time, he began throwing chunks of wood in the direction where he thought the house was. Only when he was absolutely certain one of the chunks had hit the house did he let go of the rope and follow the sound.

The storm let up on Wednesday the thirteenth. By Thursday the skies had cleared and we dared to go outside.

Snow had drifted up against our windmill to the second round, which was almost eighteen feet. The north side of the machinery shed was drifted in so that I could ride my sled down off the roof and directly onto a snowbank. It was so high in front of the house we kids slid down a ten-foot embankment to get in our kitchen door.

The road to town was completely blocked. The snowplow came out on Friday and tried to clear it. It couldn't push through. Finally, they brought out a big highway blower-type snowplow. It stalled out halfway up the hill. At the point where it stopped, the face of the drift was ten feet high.

We missed three days of school before neighbors put runners on a buckboard and came up to get us. For the rest of the winter, we had to walk a quarter of a mile down to the Namanys to catch the bus because the road stayed blocked.

When the snow melted in the spring, many farmers found their livestock standing frozen where they were standing when the storm hit. Some farmers had their herds wiped out. Because of Dad's "sixth sense" about the oncoming storm, Marks didn't lose any cattle--only a few pigs and sheep.

On Christmas morning the kids were required to stay in bed till everything was ready. We all came out together to see what Santa brought.

Dick said he had to go pee. Knowing of his urinary incontinence Mom and Dad had to let him come out. He sneaked a peek, came back and announced, "Kate, you got a doll. James, you got a wagon."

Catherine got really mad at him for telling.

Whooping cough (pertussis), with its prolonged cough, killed as many as seven thousand a year in the U.S. In April 1941 all the kids in school coughed their heads off. Some of the parents went to the doctor and suggested it might be whooping cough. But he said no. By the time the doctor admitted it was, every kid in the school had it, including the three Alexander kids.

With whooping cough, when you start coughing you can't stop. Mom put buckets beside our beds. We coughed till we threw up, then coughed some more.

We brought it home to David. He was eleven months old. Not only did he get whooping cough, he got double bronchial pneumonia on top of it. He was a really sick kid.

Mom got someone with a car to drive her and her sick child to the hospital in Spirit Lake. The doctors wouldn't keep David. They said they didn't have a contagious ward. Later, one doctor said they didn't keep him because they didn't expect him to live till they got him home. In any event, they sent the infant home to die.

Mom cried and begged if there wasn't something that could be done. One of the nurses suggested she make a tent over his crib, put a pan of boiling water laced with Vicks VapoRub inside, and keep his tiny lungs filled with vapor.

Mom was crying when she got back home. David was unconscious, blue, and barely breathing. She rigged a tent over the cook stove and put Vicks menthol in it. She held David under the tent all the rest of the day Saturday and through the night.

She refused to give up. She dragged a cot to the kitchen where she could rest. She stroked his little body, sang to him, and talked to him as if he could understand.

On Sunday night she had David lying beside her on the cot. His eyes rolled up into his head. Mom got scared. She thought, *David's dying.*

Suddenly he had an explosive bowel movement. It went through his diaper, down his legs, and all over the bed. It made a terrible mess.

That was the crisis. From that moment on, he started to get better.

David was so weak he couldn't suck his bottle. Mom dribbled milk down his throat from the end of a spoon. Dad leaned over his crib and sang, "Seeing Nellie Home," David lifted his little index finger and kept time with the music. It was then they knew he was going to get better.

David had to learn to crawl and walk all over again. He was sixteen months old before he took his first steps.

The morning of July Fourth, Dad promised to take us kids to town for the parade and celebration. But before we would be able to leave, there was a patch of hay Dad had mowed the afternoon before that needed to be raked. He told me hitch up a team and go out early that morning with the dump rake.

Mom complained that it was too dangerous for an eleven-year-old boy to be out on a hay rake alone. Dad ignored her fears and sent me out anyway. His parting instructions to me were, "Watch out for old Tom there, he seems to be pretty frisky today."

A dump-rake is a particularly wicked contraption. It has two wheels spaced about twelve feet apart. Running the full width between them is a set of curved tines that rake up the hay. The tines arch back and downward in a semicircle about three feet in diameter, points facing forward and dragging the ground. The operator sits on top.

It works like this: The operator drives across a field of mown hay. The tines gather the hay underneath the rake. When it is full he kicks a foot-lever causing the tines to raise up and dump the hay in a pile--hence the name "dump-rake." Then the cycle repeats. A good operator can get a rhythm going and dump the hay in neat windrows. This makes it easier to pick up later for storage.

I finished raking the hay without incident. The team was headed back across the pasture toward the barn when something spooked the horses. Old Tom reared up, pawed the air with his forelegs, and both horses took off running. The teeth of the dump-rake started cycling up and down, creating a hell of a racket which further added to the horses' panic.

If I had good sense, I would have jumped off the back of the dump-rake right then. But I didn't. I stayed aboard instead, trying to bring the horses under control.

They veered off to the left towards an adjacent cornfield. I yelled, "Whoa! Whoa!" at the top of my lungs, pulling at the reins, and trying to stop the runaway horses.

Suddenly the horses hit the fence. I was pitched forward. The horses veered left down the length of the barbed wire fence, one horse on each side, dragging the machine behind them. It tore out the iron fenceposts on the way.

I landed on the doubletree between the horses and the rake. I didn't dare let go because the gnashing teeth of the rake would have pierced my body and torn me to shreds. But where I was lodged was almost as bad. The flailing barbed wire cut my skin to ribbons and the horse's hooves beat a tattoo on my body. I tried to protect my face as the hay rake rolled along.

After an eighth of a mile, the harnesses were ripped off the horses and they broke free. The dump-rake came to a stop. I extricated myself from the tangled barbed wire and harness straps and began the quarter-of-a-mile treck back toward the house.

I had no idea how bad I looked. My shoes were gone, my shirt was gone, and my overalls were in tatters.

When I got to the house, Dad was in the front yard with Roland Stone, Doc Marks's other hired hand. Roland had just driven up in his car. They stared at me, speechless. I said simply, "The horses ran away."

I was a bloody mess. Almost every square inch of my body was scratched or torn. Remarkably, though, my face remained unscathed.

Roland took out his pocket knife and cut two stitches on the left side of my overalls. They fell to the ground, and I stood there naked.

Catherine ran into the house. "Mom, Mom, James is hurt."

When Mom saw me she screamed, "Oh, my God. Oh, my God."

She ran back in the house and grabbed a sheet to wrap around me. "You've got to get him to the doctor. We've got to take James to the doctor!"

Over and over again, I asked, "Is Doc Marks going to fire us?

Is Doc Marks going to fire us?" I was worried that Dad would lose his job and we would have to move again.

The chaos and panic affected five-year-old Shirley traumatically. All she could see was the horrible blood flowing from her brother. She began to cry, "Is he going to die? All of his blood is coming out!" She didn't know how they were going to stop the flow of blood. She asked repeatedly, but no one took time to answer.

The fact that Roland was there with his car was a near miracle. We didn't own a car, and much valuable time would have been lost if Dad had to run down to the Namanys or Marks to ask someone to drive me to a doctor.

I was losing blood fast. Mom became worried I might go into shock before they got me to town. Dad and Roland picked me up bodily, put me in the car--never mind the upholstery--and careened off for Lake Park as fast as the gravel road would allow.

Dr. Bullock was not in his office. He wasn't at home either. However, there was a new doctor in town, Dr. Sid Lockhart. That's where they headed next. Lockhart was a new doctor, fresh out of medical school. His office was in the front room of his house. He was at home.

Dr. Lockhart put me on the examining table. Without taking time to administer anesthetic, he started washing off the blood with alcohol so he could see how bad things were. Until then, I hadn't felt any real pain, only numbness. Alcohol brought the pain nerves back to life in a hurry.

When he had washed off the dirt and the blood, Dr. Lockhart began sewing up the worst of the wounds--still without an anesthetic. I yelled in pain. He finally gave me a shot of morphine. He said that would help ease the pain. Dad promised me his pocket watch as a reward if I wouldn't cry.

Nevertheless, the morphine was slow taking effect, and Lockhart was almost finished with his stitchery before I felt any real lessening of the pain.

Doc Marks sent me a big basket of fruit after I got home.

One of the horses had cut an artery in its leg and had to be shot.

I spent the next several weeks wrapped in bandages, looking much like an Egyptian mummy. Dad set up a day bed in the living room so Mom could watch over me while she did her housework. Once a week, she arranged for someone to take me into town so Dr. Lockhart could change the bandages.

Changing those bandages was the second most painful experience I underwent (sewing wounds without an anesthetic being the first). The gauze stuck to the wounds. No matter how carefully Dr. Lockhart tried to peel the bandages away, scabs would come off with them. I had over a hundred wounds on my right leg alone. That was a hundred scabs to tear off. Add to this the multiple wounds on my left leg, right arm, and torso, and it's no wonder I felt like a piece of hamburger.

Dr. Lockhart's bill came to $36. He never got paid. Sometime later he quietly closed his office and moved to Estherville, a much larger town.

As soon as school started, Mom got a job as a waitress in Spirit Lake, the county seat fifteen miles east. She worked nights and got paid $12 a week plus tips. To get back and forth to work, she bought a 1932 Buick sedan for $85. By working nights, she was able to be home to take care of David during the daytime.

Dad became very jealous of Mom's working. He accused her of playing around. They fought about it almost daily. Sometimes he would sneak out to check the odometer on her car to make sure she was driving straight to work and straight home again.

One night at supper they got into a terrible fight. Dad confronted her with the fact the odometer had an extra twenty-one miles on it. He demanded to know what she had been up to.

Mom flung the keys across the table at him and exploded, "Yes, Goddamn it, I drove one of the waitresses home to Spencer because her car wouldn't start. What's wrong with that? I try to do someone a favor, and I come home to get my ass chewed! Who do you think you are, God Almighty? I work all night, come home and wash your clothes and cook your food and take care of your kids, and what do I get for it? I get accused of cheating. Well, if you're so Goddamned good why don't you go out and earn some Goddamned money so I wouldn't have to?"

She slammed out the door and sat crying in the front seat of her car. When Dad wasn't looking, Catherine sneaked outdoors and took Mom a coat.

Dad's ego could not accept his wife working. It was an symbol of his failure. Several times during their towering arguments, Dad got out his shotgun and threaten to shoot someone. He never did.

It seemed as if Dad took all his frustrations out on me. Even when one of the other kids did something wrong, I became the recipient of the full force of his fury.

It seemed as if he blamed me for the loss of his dream. Down deep inside he felt that if Mom hadn't got pregnant, and if I hadn't come along, he wouldn't have had to get married and too soon take on responsibilities for raising a family. Never mind that he kept making babies, my existence was a visible reminder of all that had gone wrong in his life.

For example, Shirley was helping us kids herd the cows into the barn. We thought all the cows were in, so I closed the big sliding door. Shirley, standing on the edge of a feeding tough, reached up to slide the hook into the hasp. Someone called, "Here's another one." Immediately, the big barn door was flung back and it sliced the tip off Shirley's finger. Dad's immediate reaction was to beat the hell out of me as if it were my fault. Shirley and Catherine both cried, "James didn't mean to! It was an accident."

Dad's angry response was, "Well, next time he'll learn to be more careful!"

This occurred on a Saturday night when we had no means of getting Shirley to the doctor. She saw her blood coming out. It caused her to experience the same feelings of panic as when I had my accident.

Mom resorted to her home remedies--turpentine, Lysol and poultice. Shirley cried as Mom was pouring turpentine over her finger, "Am I going to get 'fection?" Over and over again she said, "Mom, am I going to get 'fection? Am I gonna die?"

Another episode occurred one afternoon right after lunch when Mom washed some empty fruit jars that she asked Shirley to carry down to the cellar.

To get into the cellar, one had to come out the kitchen door, cross a cement slab, and make a quick left down the cellar steps.

It happened to be one of those idle summer days farm kids know so well. There were no toys to play with, just space and each other. Catherine, Dick, and I were out in the front yard running and romping. Dick and I both carried homemade slingshots.

Shirley, in an effort to save herself a couple of trips, picked up four or five jars--more than her chubby arms could handle well. She came out the door and started for the cellar steps. She stumbled and fell on the concrete. Some of the jars broke. One piece cut her hand, nearly severing the little finger on her right hand. Blood gushed from the gash.

Dad was out by the barn unhitching the horses when it happened. He mistakenly assumed I had hit Shirley with the sling shot, causing her to drop the jars. He became irate.

He still had the doubletree in his hand from unhitching the wagon. That's a piece of oak about twice the length of a baseball bat with iron fittings on each end which are used to connect horses to a wagon.

Dad ran up and started beating me with the doubletree. He hit me on the back, arms, legs, head, any part of my body he could reach. I tried to protect myself. I ducked the swings to my head by raising my arms. That seemed only to make him madder.

Catherine screamed, "Don't hit James. He didn't do it. Shirley fell. Shirley fell all by herself."

Mom rushed out and pulled Dad off me. She said he probably would have killed me if she hadn't intervened. That's how mad he was.

Hello, Central, Give Me Heaven
Papa I'm so sad and lonely,
Sobbed a tearful little child,
Since dear mama's gone to heaven,
Papa darling you've not smiled;
I will speak to her and tell her,
That we want her to come home,
Just you listen and I'll call her
Through the telephone.
Hello Central, give me heaven,
For my mama's there;
You can find her with the angels
on the golden stair;
She'll be glad it's me who's speaking,
call her, won't you please;
For I want to surely tell her,
We're so lonely here
--"Hello Central, Give Me Heaven"
-- Charles K. Harris

9

Rejection and Abandonment

Outside the window of Catherine and Shirley's bedroom stood a cedar tree which was a favorite roosting place for a big, old hoot owl.

The night of January 3, 1942, Shirley awoke around midnight to the sound of the owl's hooting. It seemed especially mournful this particular night and filled her with a sense of dread and uneasiness.

Mom and Dad had been downstairs fighting when she went to bed. Now it was quiet.

She left Catherine sleeping and made her way downstairs. When she got to the bottom step, she saw Dad bent over the table sobbing. She knew something was terribly wrong. Her stomach felt sick. She was distressed to see Dad so upset.

Shirley went to Dad and asked him what was wrong. All he could say was, "Your Mom has left." He sobbed some more.

Feeling helpless, she went back upstairs and climbed back into bed beside Catherine. She fell asleep listening to the sound of the hoot owl. When morning came, she got up and went about her day. No one explained to her what was going on.

Over the next few days, Shirley transferred her allegiance to Catherine as "mother in charge."

Mom arranged to stay with Aunt Myrtle--widow of Mom's deceased brother Raymond--in Salt Lake City, Utah. Myrtle had found a job for her. Her plan was to save up enough money to move Dad and us kids out there. Also, she hoped that her brother Walter could get Dad a job at the Utah Copper Mine where Walter worked. The company paid $5 a day. Compared with the $1 a day Dad made on the farm, that seemed like a fortune.

After Mom left, Dad tried a succession of housekeepers. None of them worked out. The first was a high school girl, Bertha Altmeyer, who lived a couple of miles to the east and rode the same school bus as Catherine and me. Dad cleaned out his and Mom's bedroom and fixed it up nice for Bertha. He even sprayed the mattress for bed bugs.

She stayed one night. There were others.

He prevailed on Mrs. Rausch, mother of our neighbor to the north, to look after us kids during the daytime. Her grandson, Harold, was in my grade. Mrs. Rausch wasn't expected to take care of the housework, just provide an adult presence.

Granny Rausch and I did not get along. She was an old fussbudget, always criticizing, and impossible to please. I became defiant. When she picked on me, I'd sass her back. Some of our verbal exchanges got pretty hateful.

Whenever my misbehavior was reported to Dad, he'd give me a beating--not just a whipping, but a bruising beating. He'd use a piece of wood the size of a barrel stave. Other times he'd cuff me around the head.

Storefront

Doc Marks didn't like the idea of Dad living in the house with five kids and no mother. He fired him.

However, out of the kindness of his heart--or possibly pity--Doc persuaded the owner of a vacant storefront in town to let the motherless family move in there temporarily.

The storefront was the northernmost building in the business block on Main Street, on the east side. Previously, it had housed a hardware store. The front was all plate-glass windows with a door in the middle. Dad rigged up some blankets and burlap to give privacy from passersby. It was horrible, but it was a roof over our heads.

The inside of the building had no partitions. The sleeping quarters were also the living quarters. Beds were everywhere, separated only by burlap hung from clothesline. We slept two to a narrow bed. Our only source of heat came from a kitchen range located near the front of the store against the north wall.

It gave me a funny feeling to walk out the front door and be standing on the town's main street.

From somewhere, Dad came up with the sorriest excuse for a housekeeper one could ever hope to see. Her name was Opal Williams.

Opal was somewhere in the range of thirty-five to forty years old. She had a two-year old son but no husband. A shiftless boyfriend hung around the place a lot. She wasn't sure if the boyfriend was the boy's father or not.

Opal was unkempt and slovenly. She never lifted a finger to do anything unless she had to. David would fill up his pants with potty, and she'd wait for Catherine to get home from school to change him. The poor kid had diaper rash all the time.

The one thing Opal could do was talk. Her mouth ran on and on in an incessant chatter. To hear her tell it, she knew more about everything than anybody else. She didn't mind telling you so. According to her, she had a superior education, could speak French, had traveled all over the world, and knew lots of important people. The only thing she never explained was how she arrived at her current sorry state of impoverishment.

Opal had her own theories about the care and keeping of babies. She said, "If a baby's feet are warm, his whole body is warm." That's how she did it. When little David got cold, she'd prop him up in front of the oven with his feet sticking close to the opened door. After a while, if his toasted toes felt warm, she'd declare his whole body warm--no matter that his fingers and nose might be turning blue.

Dad got a job with Fred Ahrenstorff, whose farm lay two miles to the east of the Marks's place. Ahrenstorff was in the process of building a tenant house for a hired hand. Dad agreed to work without pay to finish the house so we could move into it before summer.

Our only income came from my job of setting pins at the bowling alley. I was not yet twelve. Every afternoon after school and evenings to ten o'clock or later, I labored to provide food and fuel for the family.

It was a two-lane bowling alley in the basement under the beer hall. It didn't have pin-setting machines, so the bowling pins had to be placed by hand. Tending two lanes kept me hopping. My seventh-grade teacher, Miss Holloman, thought it was terrible for a boy my age to be working in a beer joint. She was sure I would be corrupted. But as I saw it, I didn't have much choice--it was work or go hungry.

My pay was a nickel a game. Week nights I'd earn fifty to seventy-five cents, Saturday nights as much as a buck fifty.

I didn't get to keep any of the money for myself. Every bit went to support the family. For a quarter we could buy a five-pound sack of beans. Five pounds of flour was twenty-three cents. A quart of milk sixteen cents. Down at the coal yard, the manager let me pick up a gunnysack full of scrap coal that had fallen off the trucks, and only charged me fifty cents. One sack would last nearly a week. A full sack weighed sixty pounds, which was quite a struggle for me to lug the three blocks to home, uphill most of the way.

Opal Williams arranged a surprise party for my twelfth birthday on February 16. Miss Holloman trumped up a reason to detain me after school. When I got home the family all jumped out and yelled, "Surprise!" After it was over, Catherine remarked that this party was one of the nicest things that ever happened to me.

By early March, Mom had fulfilled her promise. She saved enough money to send Dad a money order in the amount of $155. That was enough to buy train tickets for us to get to Salt Lake City. Moreover, she had a job waiting for him at the world's largest open-pit copper mine at Bingham Canyon, Utah. Soon the Alexander family would be reunited again.

It never happened. Dad frittered away the money. Mom made several long-distance calls demanding to know when we were going to come out to Salt Lake. He gave her first one excuse then another. He said that the Western Union man told everybody in town he had some money. The grocery man and other creditors came with the sheriff to collect their debts. After all the bills were paid there wasn't enough left for tickets.

Mom didn't believe a word of it. This was the same old problem. Money flowed through Dad's fingers like quicksilver. He didn't have the gumption to amount to anything.

That was the straw that broke Mom's back--and her heart. She finally faced the fact Dad was never going to make anything of himself. Furious beyond description and feeling betrayed, she told Dad if he didn't get his act together it was all over between them. Under no circumstances was she coming back to live on someone else's farm.

The social workers came on March 27th. They took David and Shirley away. They transported them to Indianola where they placed them with Uncle Harry and Aunt Hazel. Shirley was almost six, David twenty-one months.

When they left, Catherine saw Dad go behind the stove, put his head against the wall and cry.

Riding in the back seat of the social workers' car, Shirley listened as the two women discussed the family's plight. It was upsetting to her to hear her family discussed in such a derogatory manner. "Tut, tut...this mother left her five kids and ran off with another man... She couldn't have been much of a mother... That baby, nearly two and not yet potty-trained...." On and on they went. Oh, how she hated them.

Shirley wondered, *Is some of my mother's pride at not accepting welfare coming out in me too?*

But her agony was not over. The social workers stopped for lunch at a town along the way. It was at the home of one of their associates. Lunch was ready when they arrived. They sat at a pretty, sunlit table. David sat on a stack of telephone books so he could reach the table. Again, Shirley had to endure stories about how awful her mother was.

David wet his pants and soaked the lady's phone books. Shirley's last bit of self-esteem was quashed when one of the social workers said, "See, what did I tell you? She didn't even potty-train her kids."

Shirley and David were welcomed into Uncle Harry and Aunt Hazel's household, but Shirley had mixed emotions. She got the impression this act of kindness afforded Hazel an opportunity to be admired by the Friends Church for "taking in her husband's kin." She felt they were a "duty." She didn't feel love.

A tall elm tree stood in front of the house, with a swing hanging from one of its branches. Shirley passed many hours swinging in that swing while her emotions began to heal.

Hazel asked, "Shirley, do you go to school?"

Shirley told her a fib. Without knowing why--possibly because she was shy and didn't want to meet a bunch of new people--Shirley replied, "No, I don't go to school yet."

One day her report card arrived from Lake Park. Hazel

confronted her. "Shirley, why did you tell me you didn't go to school?"

Shirley didn't have an answer. But Hazel displayed understanding. She said, "You've probably had so much happen to you; and since the school year is almost over, it probably won't hurt if you stay out the rest of the year. You can start first grade again next year."

Ahrenstorff's

In April, the tenant house at the Ahrenstorff's was finished, and the Alexander family--or what was left of it--moved in. The house was approximately the same size and shape as the one we lived in at Everly and sat parallel to the road.

The Ahrenstorff farm was five miles out of Lake Park, past the Marks's and two miles east. They farmed a half-section of land, 320 acres, that backed up to the Minnesota border on the north.

Freddie Ahrenstorff was twenty-five years old and a college graduate. He met his wife, Alta, while they were both attending St. Cloud State University. He a senior ag-major and she a sophomore home-ec major. She was originally from Sacred Heart, Minnesota, where the Mississippi River begins as a small stream.

Alta dropped out after her sophomore year to get married. Their son, Bobbie, was born in February, a few short weeks before we moved out there.

Uncle Harry came up on Memorial Day and brought Shirley to spend the summer. Aunt Hazel and David stayed in Indianola.

A tornado hit while Harry was there. It happened at dusk. We heard the warning siren from the water tower in town. We rushed out into the yard to see why the siren was going off. We saw a big rope dangling down out of the sky. Only it wasn't a rope, it was a tornadic funnel. We watched it come closer, then decided to run for the basement.

After hearing the all-clear, we ventured outside to look for damage. We were lucky. We saw the trail of debris where the twister tore up several A-frame hog houses in the feed lot immediately to the west but stopped at the fence just thirty feet from our house.

The next morning Harry took us for a ride to the farm of Verne Schwarzenbach, the worst hit of five farms in the area. It was a mile to the west of the Marks's. The Schwarzenbach family made it safely into the storm cellar when the tornado hit, but their home was badly damaged. Five buildings were destroyed. More than twenty animals were killed. Debris was scattered everywhere.

Dad called for Catherine and me to come over and see an unusual sight. He pointed to a six-month-old pig that had been torn apart by the force of the tornado. Its hindquarters lay in one place, its entrails and mid section ten feet away, and another ten feet beyond was the head and one foreleg. The poor beast was stretched out as if someone had hooked a tractor to its head, another to its hind feet, and yanked it apart.

Tornadoes do weird things. We saw a cow with a two-by-four run through it like a spear. A lady had been frying fish when the tornado hit; it removed the entire house but left the fish still frying on the stove. At another farm it took a baby out of its crib and placed it unharmed in a tree. It knocked the house down.

Men pitched in to aid the stricken farmers to rebuild fences and do whatever repair work could be done at once. Women gathered in the Methodist Church to cook a meal for the families driven from their homes and for the relief workers.

Shirley, now six, had been fed well at Aunt Hazel's. She was "pleasingly plump," as Dad liked to say. A chubby round-faced child with curly golden hair and an effervescent personality, she looked like a little Dutch girl. She always wore a smile.

Shirley was the only one who could tame Dad's temper. He might be ranting and raving about something, and while the other kids were looking for cover, Shirley would climb up on his lap and he'd simmer down.

One day we played in the creek below the house against Dad's orders. The water was up and he said it was too dangerous. Some neighbor driving down the road spotted Catherine and Dick playing in the water and reported it to Dad. That evening he confronted them, gained a confession, and administered a paddling.

Catherine said, "What about James, why don't you spank him? He was there too."

I tried to explain I was at the creek but didn't go in the water, that the only reason I was there was to look after Catherine, Dick, and Shirley. But it fell on deaf ears. Dad spanked me twice as hard as the other kids. "You're the oldest," he said, "and you should serve as an example to your brother and sisters."

That seemed to be the pattern of my life.

Freddie Ahrenstorff provided me with pretty steady work the summer I was twelve. I drove a tractor. The pay was fifty cents a week.

Freddie owned a brand new Oliver tractor, the first generation of a new type of farm tractors. In contrast to the stodgy and slow FarmAlls and John Deeres, the Oliver was sleek and streamlined. It had a fifth gear capable of speeds up to thirty miles an hour.

Seldom was I sent out with the tractor by myself, however. Normally I drove it when pulling another piece of machinery that required an operator, such as a hay-baler, fertilizer spreader, corn-planter, or combine.

Freddie practiced a lot of modern, efficient farming methods. He was among the first in our area to use nitrogen fertilizer. Instead of threshing machines, he used a combine. Instead of stacking hay the old-fashioned way, he used a baler. His method of farming may have required a lot of machinery, but it cut back on the number of people required.

Freddie also gave eight-year-old Dick a job at hay-baling time. He earned only half as much as I did, however.

Dick's task was to ride on a "jump seat" on the back end of the bailer. When the bales came out the chdute, they were separated by wooden dividers that had to be caught before they hit the ground and stacked back in the feed tray. It looked simple. But if Dick missed one, he had to jump off, go back to retrieve it, and run to catch up with the ever-moving machine. Meanwhile, more bales would be coming out the chute like a relentless assembly line, each dropping another divider. There were times when Dick would have his arms loaded with dividers before he caught up with the baler.

At the end of the day, Dick was too pooped to do his usual running. I, however, who had been up front driving the tractor, still had energy to spare.

One of the nice things about living at the Ahrenstorff's was they had horses to ride. We, of course, had seen cowboy movies and we sought to emulate them. We'd get on the horses, rear them up, wave our straw hats like cowboys, and yell "Hi Ho Silver."

Dad never let us ride with a saddle. He said, "If you don't cinch it tight enough--which little kids rarely can do--the saddle might slip, make the horse nervous and cause him to run away."

He added, "If that happens, you stand a chance of getting your foot caught in the stirrups and being dragged along the ground."

One Sunday the grownups went to visit folk on a neighboring farm. Catherine and I got the horses out, put saddles on them and played Cowboys and Indians in the west pasture. We raced each other back to the barnyard. Much to our surprise, the adults had gotten back earlier than we expected. We wheeled around quickly, went around to the back of the barn and pulled the saddles off, hoping no one would notice. We sauntered back into the yard as nonchalantly as possible. We thought we'd gotten away with it, but as we walked by Freddie Ahrenstorff he said real quiet-like, "Don't put the saddles on the horses again."

Another time we decided to ride like Indians did--no bridle, just knee pressure to control the horse. Catherine and I got pretty good at it. The horses accepted our guidance and did as they were supposed to.

One day Dick tried it. The horse sensed Dick didn't know what he was doing. The horse took off down the long lane towards the road. It made a sharp turn to the right and headed for the neighbors. Dick bounced off and hit his head on the cement culvert. He screamed and yelled something awful. Blood flowed profusely from a gash in his head.

Dad whipped me for teaching Dick bad tricks. He said the older kids should know better and take care of the younger ones.

The bulk of the housekeeping responsibilities fell to Catherine. Barely eleven, she was still a little girl; but she was expected to have the responsibility of an adult.

One time after mixing up a batch of bread dough, she noticed it wasn't raising. She discovered she had forgotten to put in yeast. She was in a panic. She knew Dad would be mad for wasting all that flour and stuff. She'd probably get a whipping. So she went out in the yard over by the fence and dug a hole in the ground. She buried the dough, then went back in the house and mixed up another batch. This time she made sure to put the yeast in it.

Dad rented a frozen meat storage locker in town, as did most farmers. We didn't have a refrigerator. When he went to town on Saturday nights, Dad would bring back two or three packages of meat to last through the week. Since we didn't have any way to keep the meat chilled after getting it home, he'd lay it on the cement floor of the basement because that was the coolest place in the house.

But it was not always cool enough during the hot part of summer. One time a chunk of round steak got maggots in it. Catherine knew she'd get a whipping for letting the meat spoil. She washed off the maggots and cooked it anyway. No one got sick, but it made her sick to think about it afterwards.

Catherine was on her way in from the pasture one day. As she neared the house, she saw Dick running out to meet her. In a breathless voice he asked, "Kate, Kate, when you bake a coffee cake, do you use coffee or coffee grounds?"

"Why do you want to know?" Catherine asked.

It turns out that Dick wanted to surprise the family by baking a cake all by himself. He fired up the cook stove, got out a recipe book, and set out to make a coffee cake. When the recipe called for two-thirds a cup of coffee, he dumped the grounds out of the coffee pot and put those in the cake batter.

Catherine was very considerate and didn't make fun of his mistake. That night we all ate a piece of Dick's coffee cake and told him how good it was. "A little gritty," Dad said, "but good."

Adventure is the province of youth. When not working at farm chores, it seems I was continually thinking up new feats of derring do. They may have lacked common sense, but anything was worth a try.

For example, I tried to fly off the roof of the barn one day, using bed sheets as a parachute. But the stunt didn't work. I landed on my ass and bruised my tailbone. For several days thereafter I walked gingerly and sat carefully.

July Fourth fell on a Saturday. Dad promised us kids we could go into Lake Park that afternoon for the parade and celebration. But first he needed Dick and me to go into town to pick up a few items before the stores closed at noon.

We left at eight o'clock and walked the five miles into town, arriving about ten. We bought the things Dad asked for, turned around, and walked the entire five miles home. We got back shortly after noon.

Dad and the girls were already dressed and anxious to go. As quickly as Dick and I could grab a sandwich and change from overalls into cotton shirts and slacks, we took off again on the long walk to town. It was nearly twilight when we started toward home a second time. By then, having walked fifteen miles already plus more at the fair, my legs were so tired and my feet so leaden I lagged behind the girls all the way home.

I broke my leg the last week in July. It happened on a pair of stilts. Some men visiting Freddie bet me a quarter I couldn't run across the barnyard on those stilts. Since there wasn't much I wouldn't do for a quarter, I took the bet.

Unfortunately, it had rained recently and the ground dried into big clods. One of my stilt legs caught one of those clods. The stilts splayed out in both directions, and I took a bad tumble.

Dad and Freddie were only a few feet away. "Are you hurt?" they asked.

"No, I'm okay." But when I tried to stand up, I couldn't. My right foot angled outward in an awkward direction. I tried to straighten it. It wouldn't straighten.

Mr. Ahrenstorff yelled, "Don't stand on it! It's broken."

I didn't think it was broken because I didn't feel any pain, just numbness. Nevertheless I sat back down again while Freddie examined it.

The men lifted me into Ahrenstorff's car and drove in to see Dr. Bullock. Bullock took one look at the leg and told us the large bone was broken about three-fourths an inch above the ankle joint. It was going to require surgery to set it and he didn't have the capability. He sent us to the hospital in Spirit Lake.

It was almost eight-thirty when we got there. The hospital staff had already been notified, so they wheeled me directly into surgery. A nurse told me, "We're going to put you to sleep now. When you wake up your leg will be good as new."

She put a mask over my mouth. "I want you to count slowly to a hundred. Can you count to a hundred for me?" she asked.

I thought it would be easy. By the time I got to thirty, the numbers started getting mixed up. I tried to concentrate. My mind kept drifting away.

The nurse said, "I want you to hold up your arm now. Can you hold up your arm for me?"

I had to have help. "Come on, try to lift your hand," she coaxed. It fell down. She tried again. Again it fell. Finally, through the haze I heard her disembodied voice saying, "I think you can start now, Doctor."

I experienced terrible dreams under the ether. First, I dreamed I had split my big toe with an axe. Then I dreamed someone had a saw and was sawing off my foot.

When I came to, I looked down to see the doctors wrapping my ankle tightly with gauze. It hurt. They molded a cast around it. It covered my foot and leg to my knee with only my toes sticking out.

While waiting for the cast to set, one of the doctors explained what a terrible time they had getting the bone to pop back into place. The break was too close to the ankle joint. I asked how long I had been out. "Over an hour," he said. I told him about my bad dreams. "We ran out of anesthetic," he apologized.

The anesthetic had some kind of weird affect on me. I became real silly on the trip home. I talked all the way. I told Dad and Freddie, "I want you to take an axe and chop up those darn stilts!"

Mom came back almost immediately when she heard about my accident. I was still confined to bed and not yet able to use crutches.

We kids were happy to see her. We thought maybe everything was going to work out and we could be a family again. When she talked about Salt Lake City, where she lived, it seemed like a mystical, magical place.

Mom took Shirley for a walk out by the fence. She said, "I want to take you and James out to Salt Lake with me to live; Catherine and Dick will live with your Dad. What do you think of that?"

Shirley said, "Okay." Inwardly, however, she was thinking, *I don't want to leave my brothers and sisters.*

Mom sat Catherine and me down alone and said, "You are the two oldest kids. I want to have a serious talk with you." We complied.

"How has your Dad been treating you?" she asked.

"Okay, I guess," we responded.

"What do you mean by 'Okay, I guess?' I want to know, seriously, has your Dad been treating you all right?"

We told her Dad had been getting drunk almost every Wednesday and Saturday night when he went to town. There were some Saturday nights when he didn't come home at all.

Mom wanted to know more about that. We related to her a few examples.

Mom got visibly upset when we told her Dad had been going out with Lorna Champ, a high school girl who had a reputation for being the town slut. The previous Sunday night he had gone up to Worthington, Minnesota, with Lorna, one of his drinking buddies, and another girl. Why Worthington? Buying beer on Sunday was legal in Minnesota but against the law in Iowa.

Mom knew who Lorna was and had heard rumors about her reputation. She became furious when told about Dad's relationship with her. "Goddamn," she said, "It's bad enough that he goes off drinking and leaves you kids alone. When he starts screwing around with a fifteen-year-old girl, that's too much!"

That night Mom and Dad talked until well past midnight. Catherine was afraid they'd get into a fight, and so she stayed awake listening. Dad wanted to know where Mom got her information. Mom said, "From your children, that's who!"

Dad tried to offer excuses. He said James and Catherine must have gotten things mixed up. He said that the relationship with Lorna was entirely innocent. It was purely coincidence that they attended the same party a time or two.

Mom wasn't buying it. She'd heard too many excuses before.

They ended up in a shouting match. Finally, Mom told Dad she'd sign the "God damned divorce papers." At one point, out of the clear blue, Catherine heard Mom say angrily, "Give me a piece of paper. I want to sign away the rights to my children!"

She said she wanted to take James with her but Dad wouldn't let me go. Most women would have said, "I'll take the girls, you take the boys." But Mom said if she couldn't take James she didn't want any of them!

Talk about rejection! Catherine felt plenty of it. She could halfway understand why Mom left before. It was a progression--the fights, Mom leaving, and Dad alone with the five kids. But she couldn't understand Mom leaving this second time. If Mom felt Dad was getting drunk and abusing his children, then how could she possibly go off and leave them in his custody?

Catherine felt cheated of her childhood. She went from being an eleven-year-old girl to being a little mother. She was expected to bake five loaves of bread twice a week, do the cooking, dishes, washing and ironing. Dad expected a lot from her.

No one ever asked her if she wanted the job. If she failed to do dishes or bake bread, she got a whipping. There were no after-school activities for her. She had to get home to start supper.

Mom left early the next morning. She took the bus to Indianola to visit David.

When she got there, Uncle Harry at first refused to let her see him. He said she didn't deserve to see her son. He finally relented enough to say he would bring David out to the car to see her.

Mom was allowed less than a half-hour to be with her youngest son. She held him in the back seat of the taxicab that brought her there. Finally, tearfully, she gave him back to Harry. From that point on she felt nothing but intense hatred for Harry.

Catherine cried for a week after Mom left. On Saturday night the Ahrenstorff's planned to go across the border to Jackson, Minnesota. Dad suggested they take Catherine along. Maybe the trip would help her get over her grief. But Catherine just looked out the window and cried all the way there and back. She didn't even get out of the car. Mrs. Ahrenstorff brought her an ice-cream cone.

Summer came to a close. Aunt Florence came to get Shirley. It had been decided Shirley would live a year with her.

Catherine rode the big bay horse at a full gallop up to the front porch of the Ahrenstorff house where Florence sat chatting with Alta Ahrenstorff. Catherine reared the horse up on its hind legs, waved her hat, and did her "Hi Ho Silver" routine. She charged off again. Aunt Florence almost fainted right there on the spot.

Catherine accompanied Florence and Shirley to southern Iowa and stayed a week. When it came time for her to return home, she knew she'd be leaving Shirley. She went to the outhouse and cried. When Florence found her with swollen eyes, she said, "A bee stung me." She cried all night.

Next day Catherine was scheduled to ride into Des Moines with Aunt Florence's sister-in-law, Marguerite Mitchell. Florence packed Catherine a basket of fried chicken and cookies to eat on the 200-mile train ride north.

She had to get at up four a.m. and walk a mile to Marguerite's house. Cousin Faune got up to walk with her. It had rained the night before. The roads were muddy. The girls used a flashlight to see by. Catherine cried all the way.

Dad met her up at the depot when she arrived in Spirit Lake. On the way home he stopped at a cafe and asked if she wanted a milk shake. Catherine didn't know what a milk shake was, but she said, "Okay."

"What kind?" the waitress asked.

"I don't know, what kind do you have?" She finally settled on banana-flavored, her first milk shake.

For Shirley, Aunt Florence and Uncle Raymond's home was a welcome refuge. Here was a family that functioned like a true family. Raymond was a successful farmer. Florence cooked, cleaned and mothered. She took care of the garden, chickens, and separating the cream each day. Shirley found these activities to be fascinating. Also, she had an older "brother" and "sister" to be proud of at school--her cousins Dale and Faune. She never missed an opportunity to point out her cousin Faune to her friends. Faune was so grown up and in high school on the second floor of the building. Faune endured Shirley's adulation with good humor and never lost patience.

Shirley's favorite task on the farm was gathering eggs. She loved reaching under the hens into the warm nest for newly-laid eggs. Every night as she went to bed she asked Florence to be sure to get her up early so she could gather the eggs before going to school.

Aunt Florence took Shirley along when she went to Indianola to take the cream and eggs to market. There, they would visit Grandma Alexander, now sixty four. Grandma Alexander loved children.

Florence gave Shirley lessons in social graces. Before going into town, she was made to come in from play, take a bath, clean up, and put on a dress. Florence never allowed her to wear her overalls into town. "It isn't lady-like," she said.

Living with Florence was the first time Shirley experienced life without conflict and crises. Saturday nights they ate popcorn and listened to radio dramas. They went to church on Sundays. They dressed up in gloves and hats to go to weddings and funerals. Life was good.

Uncle Raymond, a reticent Scotsman, seemed to enjoy the bouncing, energetic child who gave him a hug and a goodnight kiss each night.

To top it off, Shirley was highly praised at school. She did so well in her school work that she was often the last one standing in the Friday spelling bees. Evidently sitting out a year proved beneficial. Her first grade teacher told Aunt Florence she finished the year with the highest grade point average ever.

My broken leg caused me to miss the opening two weeks of school. Even after being pronounced fit to travel, I found it awkward getting on and off the school bus with crutches and a heavy cast. Getting up the stairs to the second floor classroom was no easy task either. I was now in the eighth grade, Catherine the seventh, Dick the third.

The cast came off the end of September. In its place, an elastic bandage was wrapped around my ankle. To provide more ankle support I wore lace-up, high-top boots and walked with a cane.

Around the middle of October, Dad became secretive about a lot of things. We kids sensed some changes were about to take place, but we didn't know what they were. Dad only said, "I can't tell you yet, but you'll find out in due time."

On the Thursday before Halloween, Uncle Harry showed up in the afternoon towing a long four-wheel trailer. It was then that Dad informed us we would be moving down to Indianola to live with Uncle Harry.

That was also when Dad gave notice to Freddie Ahrenstorff he was quitting. Freddie wasn't happy to find out this way, but he made no effort to dissuade Dad from leaving.

I tried to piece together the possible reasons for Dad's secretiveness. Two possibilities occurred to me: either Dad owed a lot of bills and wanted to get out of town, or Uncle Harry had concluded Dad had made such a mess out of things that he needed to step in and take charge.

We loaded the heavy stuff on the trailer that evening. After a cold breakfast the following morning, we loaded dishes, clothing, and personal effects.

By ten o'clock we were on the road. Another chapter in our lives had closed.

Trouble comes, trouble goes,
I done had my share of woes.
Time get better by 'n' bye.
But then my time will come to die.

10

Almost Making It

Friday, October 30, 1942

Uncle Harry didn't take the most direct route to Indianola. He turned east toward Spirit Lake. There, he wheeled up in front of the county social work office. He and Dad went in while Catherine, Dick, and I waited in the car. In a few minutes Harry and Dad came out, got us kids, and took us inside.

A social worker led us into a storeroom stacked high with numerous boxes and shelves of clothes. There didn't seem to be any particular order to the various piles. She rummaged around to find the right sizes for each child. She outfitted me with two rumpled pairs of pants--one of purple corduroy and the other blue cotton--two shirts, some underwear, and a winter jacket. I also got a pair of shoes.

Catherine and Dick were similarly attired, except that both of them were issued corduroy snowsuits. Catherine exclaimed, "This is the first snowsuit I've ever owned."

Harry had us change into our new clothes and throw our old overalls away.

For as long as Mom had been with us, the family had never participated in any welfare programs. Mom had a lot of pride. She would rather starve than ask for handouts. She said her family was made of sterner stuff than that. She felt Dad needed to learn to stand on his own two feet. She was afraid once he started accepting government handouts that would quickly become a way of life.

But Mom was gone now and Uncle Harry seemed to be in charge. Dad acquiesced.

Thus decked out in welfare clothes, we settled down for the two-hundred mile drive to Indianola. Dick rode most of the way in the front seat with Dad and Uncle Harry. Catherine and I were sandwiched into the back seat between boxes and sacks of belongings. Harry's car--a brown 1933 Chevy two-door sedan--had a bad muffler. It was smelly and noisy riding in the back seat. It was also cold, because the front windows were rolled down for ventilation.

We arrived sometime after dark. Aunt Hazel and David, now two-and-a-half, came out to greet us. Hazel had a belly-warming pot of stew simmering on the stove for us. She apologized for the other members of her family not being present. Morton was working nights at a war plant in Ankeny, Roscoe was playing high school football, and Flora had gone to the movie with friends.

Harry Alexander, born in 1897, was thirteen years older than Dad and the eldest of the five children. He stood about an even six feet tall, sturdy build, dark thinning hair with a bald spot in back. Slow moving, he gave the impression of being very deliberate. Harry was a Quaker and a rigid moralist. His moralism was tempered by a deceptive, low-key sense of humor that sometimes caught the unwary victim by surprise.

As with all the Alexander clan, Harry began life as a farmer. For the first few years of marriage he farmed the eighty acres west of town given to his wife by her father, who endowed each of his children with the same largess. But in 1933 Harry took a job with the state highway department, sold the farm to his brother-in-law, Cyrus Morton, and moved into town.

Aunt Hazel was clearly at the age of menopause, medium height, a little thick-set, graying hair styled in old-fashioned set waves, and dressed plainly as befitting a Quaker wife. She had breast cancer that started when Flora was a baby. She was under treatment in an experimental program at the University of Iowa Medical School at Iowa City. Every few months she went for more tests and treatment.

Harry was passive. He went along with whatever his wife did and said.

Their home was a large, two-story frame house on North Fourth Street, two blocks east of the highway and four blocks from the courthouse square. The house, though old and sadly in need of paint, sat on a full half city block. It had five rooms downstairs plus a laundry room, and four bedrooms upstairs. Water was pumped by hand from a well outside the back door. The outhouse was thirty yards to the east in back of a ramshackle garage.

They had four kids. Floyd, the oldest, was in the U.S. Marines stationed in the Pacific. Morton was nineteen, Roscoe seventeen--a high school senior, and Flora, fourteen. Flora was in the eighth grade--the same as me, although a year older.

We arrived the night before Halloween. Hazel put Dick and me in Morton's bed. He was working the graveyard shift in Ankeny and wouldn't be home until around nine in the morning. Catherine was put in Flora's room for the night. Around midnight, I roused enough to hear Roscoe come in noisily from his football game.

Next morning Roscoe was ranting and raving to anyone who would listen, particularly to Morton when he got home from work. The previous night's football game against Carlisle was the last game of the season and the last in Roscoe's high school career. With one minute to go and behind five points, the Indianola team ran a "naked reverse." The entire team faked a run to the left, taking all the Carlisle defenders with them. The fullback, Denzil "Diesel" Johns carried the ball to the right. As he passed the referee on his way untouched into the end zone, Diesel called out, "Hi, Ref."

The referee called the play back, hit Diesel with a penalty for speaking to an official, and Indianola lost the game.

Roscoe was still furious--not at his friend--but at the referee. He thought that was a "chicken" type of call for the ref to have made. Particularly when the outcome of the game and the season were at stake. He felt sure the ref "had it in" for the Indianola team.

Roscoe had a volatile personality. Standing five-foot-seven, stocky build, and sandy curly hair, he played at guard position on the football team. He could talk about a mile a minute--and usually did.

His older brother Morton, on the other hand, was almost the opposite--tall, lanky and taciturn. When he graduated from Indianola High the year before he was the track star. He owned a 1937 Harley motorcycle he rode back and forth to work.

Flora looked more like she could be my sister than Catherine did. Her hair was a flaming red, even brighter than mine. She was about my height and weight, but being older, she was more mature.

The downstairs of the house was divided in two parts separated by an oak "pocket" door. Our side consisted of two rooms. The large room was the "living room-kitchen area" furnished with table, chairs, and kerosene cook stove. It had a bay window with a huge Christmas cactus in it. The second, smaller room was Dad's bedroom.

Harry's side consisted of a dining room, kitchen, bedroom, and laundry room. The upstairs bedrooms were shared in common. The pocket door between the two sides downstairs remained open most of the time.

All in all, we made quite a household. Harry's side housed six people, including David. Our side encompassed four persons--Dad, me, Catherine, and Dick. Shirley was still living with Aunt Florence.

We were shoe-horned into bedrooms upstairs, which were located above Harry's part of the house. Dick and I were assigned to Roscoe's bedroom, and Roscoe temporarily moved in with Morton who would soon be moving to Des Moines to be nearer his work. Catherine shared a room with Flora.

A fourth bedroom upstairs was never used. It was furnished and had a bed that was made up all the time. Hazel called this "Grandma's Room." Grandma Alexander was presently working as a housekeeper in Des Moines. Addie Alexander was known to be an artistic, creative woman. One of the fascinating things on her dresser was a jar upon which she had glued the odds and ends of jewelry pieces. Thus an ordinary fruit jar had been transformed into a decorative piece of vari-colored orbs and globes.

Even though the house was located in the middle of town, it had no indoor plumbing. Hazel placed a tall juice can in each bedroom closet to use as a bathroom. That convenience saved us from a thirty-yard dash to the outhouse in the dead of winter. We always hoped when we got up in the middle of the night that someone hadn't already "filled the can" before we got there. If that happened, our only choices were to run it over, be miserable the rest of the night, or make the trek outdoors. The girls said it must be easier being a boy. Boys could always pee in a snowbank.

It was decided Shirley would stay at Aunt Florence's to finish the school year.

Sunday mornings found us at the Friends (Quaker) Church where Uncle Harry was Sunday School superintendent. The rule was that if one lived in Harry's house, one attended Harry's church.

Worship service turned out to be somewhat different than I had anticipated. All my life I had been told that Quakers conducted "silent" worship in which people spoke only when the inspiration hit them. But this church was more conventional. It had a paid minister, sang hymns, and preached a regular sermon pretty much like any other Protestant church.

We enrolled in our new schools the following Monday, November 2, 1942. Catherine and I both attended junior high--I in the eighth grade and Catherine in the seventh. Dick went to Hawthorne Elementary.

Indianola Junior High occupied an older, two-story building

that in earlier years had been the high school. It was a block southwest of the town square, and a block on past the new high school. From Harry's house, it was a five-block walk.

Poor Dick had to walk twice as far to get to his school. It was on the south side of town. He was a third grader.

My art teacher was Mrs. Zwick. She was a petite, prim and prissy person who styled her hair in a top-knot and wore pince-nez glasses clipped to her nose. She was not always careful how she sat. Her desk was open at the front, and often I could see all the way up under her dress. When that happened it was hard for me to concentrate on the work at hand.

Mrs. Zwick announced she would leave at the end of the year to be near her husband who was a naval officer stationed at Pensacola, Florida.

Mrs. Pickens taught eighth-grade math. Behind her back, the kids referred to her as "Old Lady Pickens." She had been there since "year one." As a matter of fact, she had taught the parents of many of the current students, and they said she was already an old lady back then.

Mrs. Pickens detested the heavy, bright red lipstick that girls wore in the 'forties. Moreover, she wasn't shy about voicing her attitude. She said it made girls look cheap and promiscuous. A pretty brunette named Mary Warner was one of the worst offenders. She always came to school with heavy layers of lipstick. Mrs. Pickens came up silently behind Mary's seat one day and clasped her head with one arm. She wiped her other hand across Mary's mouth smearing lipstick all over her face. Then she sent the mortified girl out of the room to wash her face and told her never to come back again wearing that much makeup.

The junior high principal was Mr. Townsend. He was a gangly, funny-looking, scare-crow type of person, all elbows and ears. He always wore a skinny black suit and black string tie. The boys referred to him as "One-Nut Townsend" because, supposedly, he had one testicle surgically removed on account of disease.

It didn't take long for me to get into my first fight. A ninth-grader named Butch Butler liked to bully and intimidate the younger people. Butch was a big, hulking kid. One morning on our way into the school house, Butch pushed me from behind--probably to establish his dominance over this new kid. I told him to stop. Butch shoved me again. I turned and confronted him, "I told you to stop that!"

We stood chest to chest, Butch two inches taller and twenty pounds heavier. "What are you going to do about it?" he sneered.

"I'll knock your block off!" I brazened, sticking my jaw right into Butch's face.

"Izzat so?" Butch blustered, striking me on the shoulder with the open heel of his hand. It was more of a shove than a blow.

"Yes, that's so!" I snarled back, hitting Butch's shoulder with a similar blow.

We huffed and puffed, pushed and shoved for a few seconds. Each tried to bluff the other into backing down. At length some other kids separated us. No harm done to either party. But from then on, Butch left me alone. My reputation went up considerably for standing up to him.

Unfortunately, that episode set me up as a marked man. Any kid who wanted to prove his manhood felt he had to take me on. Thus I found myself involved in a lot of schoolyard scrapes.

A further consequence was that teachers assumed if there was any rowdiness going on the classroom, like throwing spitballs, I must be involved in it. The principal's office became familiar territory. I was sent there more times than I dared count--often for things which I had nothing to do with or else was the innocent victim. There was one two-week stretch when I was sentenced full-time to the principal's office except when physically attending classes. I wasn't even allowed recesses.

Dad started work at the Swift Meat Packing Company, twenty miles away in Des Moines. I'm not sure if it was a job he applied for or one arranged by Harry. In any event, there was a war going on, and with the tremendous manpower shortage an able bodied man didn't have trouble finding a job. Dad's pay was $42.50 a week, more than he ever had before.

Dad's work was hard, smelly, dirty, and cold. He started out in the "hide room." As the beef carcasses came down the line and their hides were stripped off, the hides had to be folded into squares and stacked for later shipment to the tannery. That was Dad's job. Each hide weighed about fifty pounds, which didn't seem like a lot. But after a full day of manhandling them Dad was worn down. He wore a leather apron while he worked; nevertheless his clothes stunk to high heaven by the time he got home.

Later, Dad got promoted to being a "tailer." This job involved being stationed on the production line and cutting the tail off each carcass as it went past. The job would have been easier had Dad been taller. He had to stretch pretty high, and sometimes jump a couple of inches in the air to reach the right spot. Once, he slipped and cut himself on the arm. Another time a carcass fell on him. After those two near disasters, he went down to the blacksmith shop in Indianola and had a knife made with a curved blade and long handle so he could "tail" the carcasses without hazard to life and limb.

With his newfound prosperity, Dad bought a car. It was a black 1934 Chevy four-door. The price was $110. Its engine ran soundly, but the body had seen better days. The fenders were rusted and torn. The front bumper was loose and nearly falling off. And the vehicle rattled so loudly we could hear him coming a full block away.

With his penchant for painting, Dad painted the spokes yellow and decorated the car with twin squirrel's tails. He thought it looked "snazzy," to use his term.

On the other hand, he was such a slow driver that distances seemed twice as far as they actually were because it took so him long to get to his destination.

Dad carpooled to his job in Des Moines with four other guys who also worked at Swift's. On days he wasn't driving, he often left his car parked over by the lumber yard where the guys met.

One afternoon, My friend George Aubert and I aimlessly strolled by the lumber yard. We spotted Dad's car parked there. The keys were in it. George and I hopped in and I took us for a drive in the countryside. Since I was used to driving farm tractors, I had no difficulty driving the car.

We would have gotten away with it except for two things. First, I forgot to put the car back where I found it. Unthinkingly, I parked it at home. When the carpool dropped Dad off at the lumber yard, his car wasn't there. He thought it had been stolen. When he got home and saw it setting in the driveway, he became thoroughly befuddled. "I could swear I parked it over at the lumber yard this morning," he said. "I must be losing my mind."

Dad was about to put the episode in his "file and forget" category when the second incident occurred. During our spin through the countryside, George and I stopped to offer help to a stranded motorist. It was Leo Frazier, one of the town's two barbers. My concern was that Leo and his wife, Pauline, also happened to be members of our church.

The following Sunday, Leo mentioned to Dad, "My car broke down out west of town on Thursday. James was driving by and stopped to help. I want you to know how grateful I am."

Dad put two and two together and figured out how his car got home that day. He couldn't decide whether to be mad at me for taking the car or proud of me for being able to drive it. In any event, I escaped punishment.

When we first moved to Indianola, we secretly thought we'd be getting a mother figure--someone who would do the cooking, wash the clothes, and clean the house--and we could go back to being just kids. But it didn't work out that way.

Whether because of her illness, or by using her illness as an excuse, Hazel did very little work around the house. She was a soap opera junkie and listened to the radio all day. She loved the programs *Stella Dallas* and *Ma Perkins*.

Catherine remained as the family's "mother." At the very

least, she was the designated cook. It was a job she didn't relish. She had her share of culinary disasters, but somehow we survived. One recipe she couldn't get the hang of was how to make tomato soup. She was never able to figure out how to avoid its curdling when she added milk to the cooking tomatoes. Consequently, we learned to like curdled tomato soup.

Once a week Dad hauled the accumulated laundry off to a lady who took in washing. It was returned unironed. Ironing became Catherine's and my job. Weekly, we set the ironing board up in Aunt Hazel's living room. The iron was plugged into a lamp socket that hung down from the ceiling over the dining table on a single twisted electrical cord. That wire was the sole source of electricity in the room. A three-way socket adapter allowed us to plug in the radio, the iron, or whatever other appliance might be needed.

Dad stayed home from work one day in February, 1943, which was unusual for him. He said he had some business to attend to at the courthouse, but he wouldn't say what that business was. The mystery was heightened when Uncle Harry came home from his highway job. He changed into his good clothes and left for the courthouse with Dad.

That evening, Dad called Catherine, Dick and me together. He said we needed to have a serious talk. The upshot was our brother David had been adopted by Uncle Harry and Aunt Hazel.

We asked why. He explained that Harry and Hazel insisted if they were going to take care of David and be responsible for him, then they would have to adopt him. Dad said it was a hard decision to give up his son, but he felt this was the best way.

Dad also told us not to say anything to Mom about this in our letters. He had not informed her they were doing this, that her child was being given away, and that she would be severed from any rights of parenthood.

I wondered how they could do this. Why would the court allow a child to be adopted out without the other parent's knowledge, assent, and signature? Particularly when that parent's whereabouts were known and regular communication was maintained with her?

I came to share Shirley's view that when Harry and Hazel agreed to take David, it was more like it was their "Christian duty" than out of love. They could go to church on Sunday and impress everyone with how Christian they were.

Apparently Hazel held a "gun" to Dad's head, so to speak. She told him if he didn't agree to their adopting David, she'd see to it that all the kids were sent to an orphanage.

This wasn't the first time we'd heard that threat. Often, when we didn't behave, she'd threaten to send us to an orphanage. Catherine didn't know for sure what an orphanage was, but the way Hazel said it, it sounded like something bad. She didn't think she wanted to go there.

We felt sorry for David. He always had to wear the same clothing for a week, even his underwear. If his shorts got dirty, he turned them wrong side out and kept wearing them. Under no circumstances did he get two sets of clothes in one week, even if he dirtied them.

Throughout the 1942-43 winter months I had a job that was more pesky than profitable. Two elderly sisters, Minnie and Millie Sinclair, needed a boy to stoke their coal-burning furnace every morning and bank it every night. The pay was ten cents a day. That chore necessitated my getting up at six every morning, walking the two blocks to their house, cleaning out the ashes, and building a fire in their furnace. I came and left through a basement door, never bothering the ladies.

Getting out of bed was the hard part. Dad always made sure I was up before he himself left for work.

The job also put a damper on my night life. Around about nine o'clock each evening, I had to go back to the Sinclair house to bank the fire for the night--even if it meant leaving a movie early.

I also held a second job. On Saturdays I shoveled coal at Mayfield's Ice and Coal Company. My best friend, George Aubert, worked alongside me.

George was a likable, auburn-haired lad of Welsh descent, a

month older than I and about the same height and weight. Totally lacking in intellectual verve, he was a frequent truant from school--eventually dropping out. The classroom was not his forte. Yet he was smart as a whip and possessed a keen wit.

It was strenuous work for thirteen-year-olds. First we shoveled coal onto a truck from one of the storage piles in the yard. We then rode the truck to a customer's house where we shoveled it down his coal bin. This process might be repeated several times a day. On a busy day, we might manhandle as much as twenty tons of coal. By quitting time, my face was as black as a Kentucky coal miner's, and a white band ran across my forehead to mark where my cap kept the coal dust from settling. Often I'd have a Charlie Chaplin type of "mustache" on my upper lip where post-nasal drip cemented dark layers of coal dust.

The warming days of spring brought an end to my coal-shoveling. But I didn't lack for gainful employment. Sid Gilcrease asked me to come to work in his auto body shop, again on Saturdays. The job consisted mainly of sanding down automobile bodies to prepare them for painting. Then after the paint had dried, I buffed the cars and cleaned their interiors. Much of my time was spent doing general flunky work around the shop, which I found inordinately boring.

I lasted about six weeks before I got fired. Sid said I spent too much time watching the clock. It didn't matter; school was almost over and I would be looking for a full-time summer job.

School let out the first week in June. Dick went to Uncle Merlin's for the summer, and I went to work on the farm of Cyrus ("Cy") and Ina Morton.

Cy and Ina were Aunt Hazel's brother and sister. They lived four miles west of Indianola. Neither had married. Ina was the county treasurer and worked in town. Cy ran the farm--eighty acres left to him by their father, an adjoining eighty acres left to Ina by their father, plus the eighty acres he bought from Uncle Harry and Aunt Hazel. Adjoining them on the east was a farm owned by Brayton and Fern Harkness. Fern was another of the

Morton girls who inherited from their father. The fourth Morton girl was Lucy (Mrs. Wilson Burns) who farmed nearby.

I lived with the Mortons during the week, stayed in town on Saturday nights, and went back to the farm either on Sunday night or first thing Monday morning. Most times I rode into town with Cy but had to walk or hitch a ride back.

My wages were $4 a week and were paid directly to Dad. He, at his sole discretion, doled out only such amounts as he thought I needed. I worked about sixty hours a week as an all-around farm hand. I was expected to do a man's work from dawn to dusk throughout the planting, haying and harvesting seasons. Of course, there were animals to feed, cows to milk, and barns to clean.

The end of summer brought to a close the peaceful period in Shirley's life. She was now seven. It was her choice.

Aunt Florence talked to her one day as they were gathering eggs, "Shirley, your Dad and brothers and sister are all living down here now. This means you can go back to live with them. But Uncle Raymond and I would like for you to be our little girl, if you want to. You will have to decide where you want to live."

Shirley was torn by the choice. She was excited about the prospect of living with her dad, brothers and older sister. But she loved her new home, too. She wondered, *Maybe I could do both, live with Aunt Florence half the time and with Dad half the time.* So she asked, "Can't I do both?"

Florence replied, "No, you'll have to choose."

It was a tough choice for a seven-year-old to make. But the more she thought of her dad, she decided she wanted to be his little girl again. So she made the decision to live with him.

When the day came to leave, Florence packed her things, drove her into town where the rest of us lived. We were reunited as a family.

It was a tough row Dad tried to hoe. Every day when he came home from work, even before he could get out of the car, Hazel would meet him in the driveway. "Your kids did this..." or

"Your kids did that...."

He tried to enforce discipline with us kids while keeping peace with his brother and his wife in whose house we were living.

Hazel developed a particular antipathy towards me. I never figured out why. It didn't make any difference which kid did wrong, she'd tell Dad that I did it. Dad, in turn, would give me a whipping--maybe not every day, but at least once a week.

Catherine observed, "I think Hazel probably gets her jollies watching us get beat."

On occasions when Dad didn't beat us kids, Hazel appeared disappointed and would chastise him for not properly disciplining his children.

None of us kids ever wanted to get spanked by Dad. His anger could result in a severe beating. One day, for example, he claimed someone had stolen the meat pies he bought for his lunch. No one owned up to the crime. He announced that the guilty party would have one more chance to come forward and spare the other kids a beating. When no one admitted guilt, he lined us all up in a row. He grabbed a sawed-off broom handle that Catherine used to practice baton twirling. Starting with the oldest, me of course, he gave a dozen whacks. Catherine got maybe half that many. Dick got three and Shirley one.

That broomstick beating was probably the worst Catherine ever got. Dad had a baseball pitcher's arm. When he reared back and let go, it felt like hitting a home run. It hurt so bad that she was still crying at nine o'clock that night. Yet her blows were just a fraction of the number I got.

Later, Shirley said something about it to Dad. He replied, "Well, I knew you hadn't taken them, so I just gave you a little spanking."

But whether she got a spanking or not, Shirley couldn't stand violence. Many times she begged Dad not to give me or Dick a spanking. Dad said Shirley was so sensitive all he had to do was look at her cross-eyed and she'd cry.

For Shirley, the best part of living at Uncle Harry's house was she now had little brother David back, so to speak. At least they were living under the same roof.

David was hungry for someone to play with. "Tootie, Tootie, come out and play with me," he would beg. They played hollyhock dolls together, swung in the swing, and climbed trees.

One day Shirley and David were playing tag when she noticed that a sweater Hazel washed had fallen on the ground. She tried to put it back on the line. The clothesline was too high for her to reach. She climbed up on a sawed-off limb. Meanwhile, David was pulling on her legs, saying, "I want to, I want to."

Shirley slipped and came down a-straddle the sharp end of the limb. She severely cut herself on her inside thigh where her body joined her leg. Seeing blood gushing out, she ran to the house screaming for Aunt Hazel. Doc Trueblood sewed her up and said to stay off her feet a couple of weeks until time for the stitches to come out.

A couple of months later, David had an accident. He and Shirley were out back roughhousing and rolling down the hill toward the crabapple tree. Somehow David fell into the tree and broke his collarbone. Hazel said it was all Shirley's fault. She accused Shirley of being mad at David for causing her to hurt her leg. Shirley knew she hadn't done anything to hurt her brother, no matter what the grownups thought.

As Shirley began to make friends at her new elementary school, she ran into a recurring embarrassment. Whenever she got close to someone, invariably they wanted to know about the strange living arrangement of her family. "Where is your mother?" they would ask.

Shirley was too embarrassed to say that her folks were divorced. Instead, she would tell them her mother had died. That little lie generated sympathy for her. They would pity her if they knew the truth, and she'd had enough pity. She didn't want to be different any more.

None of us kids liked the way Dad's relatives talked about our mother. One Sunday afternoon Dad took us to visit Aunt Linnie and Uncle Roscoe in Des Moines. These were Grandpa Alexander's sister and her husband, and thus our great aunt and great uncle. They were childless.

The grownups talked as if we kids were deaf. They were talking about Mom. Aunt Linnie said something like, "It is terrible for a woman to give birth to five kids and then go off and leave them."

Catherine had all she could stomach. She marched up to Linnie and said, "Well, she did more than you did. She gave birth to five kids; you didn't give birth to anything!" She was *persona non grata* for a while after that.

I stood five-foot-eleven and weighed 147 pounds when I entered ninth grade that fall. At age thirteen, I was already bigger than Dad.

I was also bigger than most of the high school football players. Three weeks into the season, the coach moved me up from the junior high team to scrimmage with the varsity.

Indianola High, whose colors were purple and gold, issued each scrub player an old-style, leather helmet type of uniform. They only had enough of the new uniforms to outfit the varsity. Decked out in my scrub uniform, I looked like something from the 1920s.

As luck would have it, in the fourth game of the season, Bob Houghtaling, first-string right tackle, broke his leg. Coach moved me up to fill that position. I played the remaining six games and accumulated enough playing time to earn a letter at the end of the season--the only freshman to "letter" that year.

While still in the midst of football season, I was given a morning delivery route for the Des Moines *Register and Tribune*. That meant I had to get up at four-thirty in order to be at the newspaper office by five. The first few minutes were spent folding newspapers and stuffing them into my carrier bag. Then it was off to make deliveries. By six-thirty I was finished and headed back home where I piled into bed for another hour's sleep before school. Sometimes I overslept and was late to my first class.

I walked the route the first few weeks until I saved up enough money to buy a second-hand bicycle. The bike's brakes didn't work, so I learned to slow it down by sticking my foot up against the front wheel. One morning I accidentally caught my toe in the spokes and flipped the bike over frontwards, applecart over teakettle.

Besides getting gravel ground into the palms of my hands, which was quite painful, I bent the front fork of the bike backwards. The wheel rubbed up against the frame making the vehicle no longer ridable. I pushed the bike along the route for a few blocks, and then a brilliant inspiration hit me. I turned the wheel around backwards, and it no longer rubbed the frame--although it looked weird to see the handlebars pointing frontward. After I got home, I turned the handlebars around to match the wheel. That way I didn't have to cough up five dollars for a new fork. I dubbed the strange-looking contraption my "bass-ackwards bike."

Relations between me and Dad went progressively downhill. Nothing I did seemed to please him. He became increasingly abusive.

One continuing bone of contention was my hair. I was blest--or cursed, as the case may be--with an unusually thick head of red hair. It was so thick it resisted being combed into waves unless I let it grow longer than usual. Moreover, I was developing an interest in appearing attractive to the opposite sex. As a case in point, one female teacher, seeing my head bent over my desk, remarked, "It's a shame to waste hair like that on a boy."

Compliments like this had no affect on Dad. He continued to ridicule my hair and sarcastically refer to it as a shaggy mane.

Whenever I was with Dad, it was always, "James, do this," or "James, do that." I resented his trying to control my life so tightly. I wanted a little slack. Most of the time, I kept silent. Sometimes I would walk out. Every once in a while, though, I would get fed up with being called "lazy," "shiftless," "worthless," or "irresponsible," and I would sass back. When that happened, all hell would break loose.

Dad had a habit of slapping me across the face with the back of his hand. If I raised my arms to defend myself, that made Dad even madder and he might start using his fists.

One evening shortly after my fourteenth birthday, Dad started berating me over something I had apparently done to raise his ire. I sassed back. Dad approached me in a menacing manner, "Don't you dare talk back to your Dad, or I'll take you outside and beat you within an inch of your life!"

I was by then over six feet tall and weighed a hundred-ninety-five pounds. When I stood up, I towered over him by several inches and outweighed him by fifty pounds. I said, "Okay, let's do it! You wanna fight, let's go out on the porch and get it over with."

Dad blustered, ranted and raved, but he never stepped out onto the porch to meet the challenge. Indeed, from that point on, he stopped using--or even threatening to use--physical force on me.

That didn't mean the war was over, however. It merely shifted ground. Dad resorted to more intensive verbal abuse.

My attitude changed as a result of this confrontation. I decided I was big enough to take care of myself now and I didn't need Dad anymore. I declared my emotional independence and no longer let his rantings and ravings bother me.

The summer of 1944, I worked at Crittendon's Produce Plant. The company's main business activity was to buy milk, cream and eggs from farmers and process these into pasteurized milk, butter, and other dairy products for retail sale in grocery stores.

I tossed a lot of ten- and twenty-gallon steel milk cans around that summer. These cans weighed 120 and 240 pounds, respectively, when full of milk. The good thing about it was that the strenuous activity helped to bulk me up for football that fall. I finished the summer at 205 pounds.

I learned to candle eggs--a procedure for testing whether an egg is fertilized, rotten, or otherwise defective. Crittendon's took in a lot of eggs. Whenever other work was caught up there were always eggs to be candled.

My pay was $12 for a six-day work week, including working

until ten or later on Saturday nights.

Some friends told me I was foolish to work for only $12 a week at Crittendon's while I could be "tasseling" corn for $20 a week. It sounded like a pretty good idea, so I handed in my resignation.

Tasseling is a process used on farms which seek to develop new strains of hybrid corn. The process works like this: (a) alternate rows are planted with different strains of corn, (b) pollination takes place when the tassels reach a certain maturity; so (c) to prevent unwanted cross-pollination, the tassels are pulled off rows "A" before they start shedding pollen and leaving only rows "B" to carry on the genes to the next generation.

I soon realized I made a mistake. We started out early in the morning while the corn was still wet with dew. By nine o'clock my clothes were soaking wet from walking down the rows of head-high corn. Then as the sun climbed higher the heat started beating down, causing the corn to exude great quantities of moisture. By eleven o'clock, the whole field turned into a sweltering steam bath.

I did that only a few days. When I found out my job was still open at Crittendon's, I bid adieu to the profession of corn tasseling.

Mr. Crittendon gave me an opportunity to increase my earning power. I could go into business for myself, so to speak.

There was a lean-to shed on the north side of the building where they assembled wooden egg crates. I was to be paid on a piece-work basis--a nickel for every crate I assembled. I did some quick mental calculation and figured if I could assemble a crate in five minutes, that would be twelve crates an hour. At five cents a crate, I would earn sixty cents an hour, or $24 a week. That was twice what I was making now. I took the job.

The parts were all prefabricated. All I had to do was fit the pieces together in a jig, and nail them. I'd toss the finished crate onto the stack, and go on to the next.

Taking that job was a good move on my part. I found I had to keep at it--no goofing around--but I could maintain the pace I set for myself. The extra money wasn't bad, either.

The county fair came to town in August. I saw an ad in the paper soliciting teen-age boys, sixteen and over, who wanted to earn extra money. The job would be for one day only, helping to set up the rides and carnival equipment.

It looked like a pretty good deal to me, so I trotted out to the fairgrounds and made an application. I lied about my age. I ended up helping set up the merry-go-round. Until then, however, I hadn't realized how much hard work went in to assembling a piece of carnival machinery.

I hung around evenings during the run of the fair. The owner let me work on the ride, take tickets, and be a general flunky.

The fair ended and it came time for the carnival to move on. The operator asked me if I wanted a permanent job. I said yes.

I left town that afternoon with the carnival.

We traveled all night and set up again the next day in Quincy, Illinois, just across the Mississippi River from Keokuk, Iowa. I found working in a carnival to be fun. There was a lot of camaraderie amongst the "carnies."

It all came to an end in just two days, however. The county sheriff came to bring me back. Not surprisingly, he had linked my disappearance to the carnival having left town on the same day. It wasn't hard to track me down.

Oddly, I suffered few repercussions from my having run away. The sheriff gave me a stern lecture, but Dad was pretty subdued. Harry and Hazel stayed out of it. My paper route and job at Crittendon's were still waiting for me.

I weighed in at the start of the football season at 207 pounds and stood six-foot-one in height. There was little doubt I again would be a starter. I stayed at right tackle, while Bob Houghtaling, the injured player I replaced last year, was moved over to left side of the line.

During preseason, we held a couple of scrimmages against Simpson College, just a few blocks down the street. The college guys were bigger, faster and more experienced, but our coach felt these scrimmages would be good for his boys.

During the second of the two scrimmages, I made a tackle against the Simpson halfback. The impact knocked me silly--the only time I was ever knocked out in a game. The college kid was being carried off on a stretcher. Word came back to us he had a broken leg.

We did not have a good football season. Indianola High finished the year with two wins and eight losses.

The only teacher I felt really understood me was Miss Ada Harvey. She was a distant cousin and my tenth grade algebra teacher.

Algebra itself was easy. I could do the problems in my head. Homework was my downfall. I detested the boring task of working out the problems in full form when I already knew the answers.

Miss Harvey worked out a deal with me: If I could work all the problems in my head without ever resorting to scratch paper, then I would not have to write them out in full form. On the other hand, if I resorted to using scratch paper even once, I was honor bound to write out the whole assignment in long form.

She trusted me, and I reciprocated that trust. Only twice during the entire year did I have to write out the problems.

Another teacher whom I liked was Harry Grange, the high school principal. He substituted for Miss Harvey a few times when she was ill or attending a conference. Grange was impressed with my quick response to questions in class, and he began to call me "Plato." The name stuck.

If all the teachers had been as understanding and supportive as Harvey and Grange, I might have enjoyed school. As it happened, I found most of the studies tedious, uninteresting or irrelevant. I did only the minimal amount necessary to get by.

When football season ended, I took a job at Stump's diner. I still carried my paper route. Stump's was located on the highway two blocks east of the town square.

The diner was a popular gathering place for the coffee-and-hamburger crowd. Fred and Maude Stump also owned a full-service restaurant on the square. Maude was a diabetic and had to take insulin shots.

Working hours were from six-thirty to eight-thirty every morning, plus another two hours after school. That meant I had to go directly from my paper route to work at the restaurant.

Cigarettes were a highly prized item during World War II. Due to wartime shortages, an unofficial form of rationing came into existence. Stump's, like most establishments, received a daily quota. Fred gave first priority to regular customers, limiting them to one pack per customer. His only exception was to the employees: we were allowed to buy two packs.

When I first started working there, I'd take my daily ration. One pack went to Dad, the other I'd sell at school. Being a source of cigarettes helped boost my campus popularity.

Over time, however, the routine changed. I took up smoking, and my buddies got cut out of their ration. Later, as my habit grew, Dad's supply got cut, too.

As long as Dad lived under Harry's roof, he was obligated to attend Harry's church. But church-going didn't really suit Dad's temperament. Almost inevitably he would fall asleep during the sermon and start snoring. We learned not to sit close to him.

Catherine asked him one time, "Is it the sermon that puts you to sleep?"

"No," he replied. "Right before they pass the collection plate I fall asleep."

One of the church women, Mary Alice Smith, took a shine to Dad. She had been our eighth grade English teacher. Mary Alice was a middle-aged, thickset, cat-loving spinster who wore horned-rim glasses. She would sidle down the pew towards Dad and try to save his soul. It never worked.

As destiny would have it, Dad did meet his second wife at the

Friends Church. Her name was Roxanne "Roxie" Nearman, a nineteen-year-old education student at Simpson College who had come to the church for a Sunday evening social. Soon she and Dad were double-dating with another couple.

Roxie was medium height, stocky build, tightly curled red hair, wore heavy glasses, and had a nervous laugh she used to cover embarrassing moments. Her mother was a school teacher in Earlam, Iowa, just a few miles west of Des Moines. Her father had been killed when she was a young child.

Shirley accompanied Dad and Roxie to a church gathering in Des Moines. She offered Roxie a bite of the dessert she was eating. Roxie declined, saying, "No, I'm afraid it doesn't like me."

Shirley was a precocious child. She shot back, "Well, my Daddy likes you." This provoked uproarious laughter among the grownups.

Soon after that, during the first week in February, 1945, Dad and Roxie got married. My new stepmother was barely four years older than I.

This turned out to be the second time we kids were disappointed in not getting a "mother." Roxie was not cut out for the job of mothering five kids. She couldn't cook, didn't sew, and wouldn't do laundry. So things continued pretty much as before with Catherine doing most of the cooking and domestic chores.

April 12, 1945, President Franklin Roosevelt died. That was Shirley's ninth birthday. It seemed like everything happened on Shirley's birthday.

The war in Europe ended three weeks later.

For some time I had been giving serious thought to leaving home again. This time for good. I had my fill of school, Dad, Roxie, and everything else.

A month after the school term ended, I sold my bike for $20. I walked to the edge of town, hitched a ride, and took off for freedom--wherever that might lead.

It's a hard row that my poor hands has hoed.
My poor feet has traveled a hot dusty road.
Out of your Dust Bowl and westward we rolled,
And your deserts was hot and your mountains was cold.
--"Pastures of Plenty"

11

Pastures of Plenty

Dad showed little emotion when told of my departure. He merely said, "Well, he's gone again." To him, it was no big deal. I had run away before, so this came as no great surprise. He figured his son would be coming back in a couple of days.

Catherine reacted differently. After several days passed and it became clear I was *not* coming back, she felt a profound sense of loss. From that time in South Dakota when I took her out on the field trip and we got lost, we had been best friends. Likewise, when our folks separated and Shirley went to Florence's, David to Harry's, and Dick to Merlin's, the two of us were always together. Now, her thoughts were, *God, how am I going to get along? I depended on you. You left me. How could you do that?*

She was also miffed because I, being very good at math, had promised if she signed up for algebra I'd help her. She was really counting on it. Now I wasn't there to make good on my promise.

Catherine had hoped that Roxie would relieve her of some of her responsibilities. But things didn't work out that way.

Roxie's mother was a school teacher. She never took time to teach her daughter anything about cooking or housekeeping. For example, if Roxie was sweeping the floor, she'd sweep around in little patches rather than sweep the whole floor. Or in preparing a meal, she might throw a chicken and a few potatoes in a pot, and when mealtime came she'd serve them--done or not. If the chicken was done, fine. If not, fine too. If she was baking a cake and didn't have milk, she'd use water. To her, liquid was liquid.

That was particularly galling to Catherine whose own mother could make a meal out of scraps or a Cinderella dress out of a kitchen curtain.

Dad was promoted to inspector at the packing plant, a position which paid a decent money. Unfortunately, he contracted a disease of the lungs called "Malta Fever" as a result of his working inside a meat freezer all day. His illness meant he could no longer work inside a freezer compartment. He was out of work for several months.

Catherine got a job at Shannon's Cafe on the east side of Courthouse Square. This made her the third generation to have worked there. Both Mom and Grandma Gamble had previously waited tables there when it was known as Berkeys.

It was hectic. Catherine would take off running from high school when the noon whistle sounded, cross the square, dash into the restaurant, and work the lunch hour. She'd run back to school at one o'clock. After school she worked until eight or nine at night. All her wages and tips went into the pot to support the family's needs.

Dad liked the idea of getting something for nothing. He'd go to auctions where he could buy things for little money, and repair and paint them for resale. He seldom made enough money to compensate for the labor he put into these projects. That didn't deter him.

One day he brought home a metal baby crib and parked it out in the front yard. Each evening he'd go out and daub a little paint on it--one slat pink, one blue, and so on. Passersby, seeing the crib, jumped to the inference that Roxie was pregnant. Since Dad and Roxie hadn't been married very long, people started circulating rumors that they "had" to get married--which was untrue.

Shirley had received a doll bed the previous Christmas. It was very precious to her, particularly since Dad did not usually buy "frivolous" toys. Mostly Dad's idea of a present was to buy clothes and other things the kids needed. But someone at the packing plant made these little "double-decker" doll beds on the side. Dad got one for her while he still worked there. She kept it stored under a table in the kitchen area.

One day she was going over to a very special friend's house to play after school and she wanted to take her prized possession along to show. She loaded her doll bed in the wagon and pulled it over there--knowing full well it was a forbidden act. After playing dolls a while, the girls played outside. Time went by faster than they realized. Shirley knew that Dad would already be home by the time she got there.

That put Shirley in a quandary--how to get her doll bed home without Dad seeing her. She went home without it, hoping for a more opportune day.

Days passed, and the girls played dolls over at the friend's house. One day Dad noticed the doll bed missing and asked where it was. Shirley made up an answer on the spot, "It--it must have been stolen."

Now she couldn't bring it home without having to admit to a lie. In her heart she knew her precious doll bed was gone forever.

Hazel kept a switch on the table within arms reach. If David so much as put his big toe out of the yard, she would yell at him about running away and start beating him on the legs with the switch.

One time Catherine heard David scream like he was being killed. She opened the sliding doors leading to Harry's part of the house and went flying out to the kitchen. There stood David, blood spurting from his nose, Hazel beside him. Catherine asked what happened. She was told it was none of her business. "David belongs to us now," Hazel asserted.

Later Catherine learned that David had opened a loaf of bread on the wrong end, and Hazel hit him so hard she broke the cartilage in his nose.

Catherine felt a mothering instinct towards David. She was nine when David was born. He was her own little doll. When he was sick she helped take care of him. When Mom went to work she took care of him. When Mom left, she took care of him. Then Harry and Hazel stepped in and took her baby brother away from her and she felt they mistreated him. She had a hard time backing off just because some old judge signed a piece of paper.

One Sunday afternoon Morton and Flora--each recently married--were there with their respective families, ten or twelve people in all. A dispute arose among the kids over possession of a softball bat. David, naturally, was the one in the wrong. Hazel came over, grabbed the bat, and whacked him one with it.

Catherine charged over and gave Hazel a piece of her mind. Morton informed, "Mama is David's mother now, and you have nothing to do with him."

Catherine began crying. She told Morton, "The only reason she wanted David was so she'd have someone to beat on."

She grabbed Shirley up and they went down the road, not knowing where they were going, and not having as much as a dime in their pockets. A lady down the street named Bernice Burrell took them in.

In the fall of 1945, Dad moved his family to a four-room crackerbox house on Clinton Street, six blocks southeast of Harry's. The rent was $10 per month.

The house was poorly heated. The girls had only one blanket each, so during the winter they put newspapers on their beds to keep warm. But the papers kept falling off.

As part of his treatment for Malta Fever, Dad was told to drink goat milk. He bought a goat which he staked out in the front yard. That led to an unforeseen consequence.

Various people would come by, see the goat, and say, "By the way, I've got a couple of goats I'd like to get rid of." Before long, Dad had a half-dozen goats in his yard. Some he milked, and some he butchered.

Money continued to flow through Dad's hands like water through a leaky dike. He just couldn't get the hang of hanging onto it. For example, he ran up a bill at Squire's Grocery Store which he couldn't pay. Catherine stepped in. Out of her meager pay at Shannon's, she paid $10 a week on it.

She would have been better served if she had spent the money on a new winter coat. The one she wore was held together by safety pins. But she was never able to keep back enough money from her wages at Shannon's to buy one.

Dad went to work at the gas station down by the Sale Barn. It was a part-time job evenings, pumping gas, changing tires, odd chores. At least it brought a few more dollars into the family kitty.

The Sale Barn Cafe advertised for a fry cook and a dishwasher. Roxie took the cook job, and Catherine took the dishwasher job.

Roxie's lack of cooking skills made her an unlikely candidate for the job. She'd panic if she got more than two or three orders behind, and someone had to step in and help her. The heaviest rush came right after the movie let out. On those occasions, they might get as many as thirty orders in rapid succession.

One night the orders poured into the kitchen so rapidly that Roxie couldn't handle the rush. She threw up her hands and ran screaming out the back door.

Shortly after that episode, Catherine left the dishwashing job and took over the stove. At age fourteen, she became the fry cook. Roxie moved up front as a waitress.

Catherine knew only one way to cook--"well done." That went over just fine with the farmers because that's the way their food was served at home.

She cooked Friday and Saturday nights till midnight. The rest of the week she worked from after school until nine p.m. Her school work slipped, but the family never lacked food. And she saw to it the family had a Christmas.

Roxie's going to work had unintended consequences. The same accusations Dad had previously leveled against Mom, he now made against Roxie. He accused her of playing around with the truck drivers that frequented the cafe. As far as Catherine knew, there was no truth to the accusations. Dad simply could not handle the idea of his young, attractive wife working around those good-looking young studs.

Shirley unwittingly played a mean trick on Dick that Christmas. She accidentally discovered what Dick was going to be getting for a present. She was made to promise not to tell. She enjoyed knowing something Dick didn't know. As the days got closer, however, she couldn't resist teasing him, "I know what you're getting for Christmas. I know what you're getting for Christmas."

She refused to tell him outright. But Dick was nobody's fool. He suckered her into playing a game of clues. Eventually, he wormed so many clues out of her that he correctly guessed what he was going to get for Christmas--a pair of long underwear.

Dick was crestfallen to "know" he wasn't going to get anything special. Shirley felt ashamed of herself, and sad for him.

This was the family's first Christmas without me. I'd been gone over five months now, they hadn't heard anything from me, and my name was no longer mentioned on a regular basis. Nevertheless, Catherine mused, *I wonder where James is tonight? Will we ever see him again?*

Dick made up for his disappointment at receiving a pair of long johns by asking Dad, "Can I have James's rifle?"

Dad said, "Yes. He's not here. He has no ownership of anything in this house."

I'm spending my nights at the flop-house,
I'm spending my nights on the street.
I'm looking for work, and I find none.
I wish I had something to eat.
Chorus:
Soup, soup, they give me a bowl
of soup, soup, soup,
They give me a bowl of soup.
--"The Soup Song"

12

Movin' On

The sun was coming up on Friday morning, July 6, 1945, when I left Indianola. I carried only a small cardboard valise, which I had hidden the night before, and $38 in cash. After finishing my paper route, I hitched a ride into Des Moines.

I wandered around the city all morning, not quite sure what to do. I caught the streetcar to the Riverside Amusement Park and spent the afternoon hanging around and riding the rides. That experience began to pall. I decided to get out of Des Moines because sooner or later my absence would be reported to the police and they would look for me.

I checked the Greyhound depot. A bus was leaving for Omaha, Nebraska, at 11:10 p.m. The ride would last five hours, which meant I could sleep on the bus. I bought a one-way ticket costing $1.56.

I waited nervously around the terminal. Every time a policemen walked by, my heartbeat increased. I could never be sure whether they were looking for me or just making a routine patrol. The waiting seemed interminable. Finally, the bus was announced and I hastened to get aboard.

Before I could breathe a sigh of relief, however, two more policemen strolled by. They looked over the passengers. I tried to feign indifference. If they were looking for someone, apparently it wasn't me, for they soon ambled on.

Omaha was a scary city. I didn't know anyone there. I didn't have the faintest idea what I was going to do there. I only knew I wanted to get away from Indianola. I had a vague idea of finding a job, but the city was too intimidating. I decided to find a smaller city.

Hiawatha, Kansas, appeared to be a likely prospect. It was a county seat town about the same size as Indianola. Just across the border from Nebraska, it was tucked into the northeastern corner of the Sunflower State. I took the night bus.

It was now Sunday. Nothing much was going on. Hiawatha didn't appear to have much to offer. I spent most of a boring day hanging around a downtown lunch counter.

I made the acquaintance of a couple of locals about my own age. They told me this was a dying town. They said they couldn't wait to get old enough to leave on their own. That was enough to convince me that I needed to move on.

A truck driver at the restaurant overheard me say I was looking for work. He said job prospects would be better in St. Joseph, Missouri, about a hundred miles to the east. He was heading that way and offered to let me ride along to keep him company.

We arrived about nine that evening. The trucker dropped me off near the bus station. The station was closed, so I wandered around until I found an abandoned building to sleep in.

I didn't like the looks of St. Joe. Monday morning found me back on the road with my thumb stuck out, seeking a ride.

Where to? Well, somewhere in the back of my mind I remembered hearing that Arkansas had a legal working age of fifteen. I figured if I could get down there I would be able to get a work permit. So I headed for Arkansas.

But I perceived a problem. The road from St. Joe to the Arkansas border ran through Kansas City. That was a huge, sprawling metropolis, bigger than Des Moines or Omaha. I feared

I would have a terrible time hitch-hiking through all that traffic, so I sought a way of going around it.

When I got as far as Excelsior, Missouri, I struck out on a secondary road that bypassed Kansas City on the east. That turned out not to be such a good idea. Traffic was light, and most of that was local. I walked, sticking my thumb out at an occasional passing car. A few, mostly farmers, gave me a short ride.

By mid-afternoon I had only gotten as far as the east-west highway between St. Louis and Kansas City. I had traveled only twenty miles, and I figured I'd walked half of that. I was thoroughly pooped. Time to rethink my strategy.

Instead of continuing on south past the eastern edge of Kansas City, I decided maybe I could navigate the big town after all. I turned west.

The driver of a gravel truck picked me up. The truck was empty because he was through hauling for the day and on his way home.

Passing through Independence, the trucker proudly remarked that this was President Truman's home town. I nodded. He asked if I'd like to see the President's house? I said yes.

The driver detoured a half-dozen blocks off the highway and traveled down a residential street. He pointed to a modest, white two-story frame house. "That's where the President lives," he said.

It was not an impressive edifice. I expected to see a security fence and guards surrounding it, but there were none.

I was more interested in finding a place to stay for the night. The trucker suggested a men's hotel that he was familiar with. He said it wasn't anything fancy, but it was clean, private, and cheap. I assented, and he dropped me off there.

The "hotel" turned out to be a flop house in a seedy district on the edge of downtown Kansas City. With considerable trepidation, I went in and inquired about prices.

Rooms were seventy-five cents, plus a refundable key deposit of fifty cents. I counted out the money from my dwindling supply and went upstairs to find my room. I wish I had seen it before I paid out my money. The room was a little cubicle on the second floor, barely the length of a single cot and hardly wider than the bed. The only furniture was a hard-backed chair and a couple of hooks to hang one's clothes. The partitions between the cubicles were about seven feet high and open at the top. Consequently, noises from dozens of such cubicles carried throughout the cavernous structure.

I was frightened. My imagination ran out of control. It conjured up all sorts of awful things that might happen to me, such as being raped or robbed. Tired as I was, I couldn't go to sleep. After a couple of hours trying to shut off my mind, I went downstairs, got my key deposit back, and walked into the night.

A dozen or so blocks west of the hotel I came upon an older, rundown residential neighborhood. I found an unlocked car and curled up for the night in its back seat. Somehow, I felt a lot safer there than back at the flop-house hotel.

Next morning I resumed my journey southward towards Arkansas, nicknamed the "Land of Opportunity." I took the streetcar to the end of the line, then started hitchhiking.

I got only as far as the town of Belton, about twenty-five miles south. The local police picked me up and hauled me off to jail. It took three days for them to turn me loose. No charges were filed. Apparently they were just checking out vagrants.

It was now Friday afternoon. I had been gone a week. I was tired, discouraged, and nearly out of money. Things were not working out the way I had thought they would. So when I took my leave of the Belton jail, I headed back north with the vague idea I might go home again.

Nightfall found me at Cameron, Missouri, a crossroads town about halfway between Kansas City and the Iowa border. I slept behind a billboard on the north edge of town.

When morning came, I hooked up with a trucker at the little restaurant across the road. He said he was going to Carroll, Iowa, northwest of Des Moines.

Initially, I planned to ride only as far as Indianola, but the closer we got the more apprehensive I became. I didn't relish the idea of facing Dad--or, for that matter, Harry and Hazel either. So by the time we got to five-mile corner where Highways 65 and 69 join, my mind had changed and I told the driver I'd ride all the way to Carroll with him. I thought perhaps I might go on up to Sioux Falls, South Dakota, and connect up with Mom's relatives, the Websters.

It was dark when I got to Sioux Falls. I hadn't the faintest idea how to contact the Websters. Moreover, I didn't know what I'd say to them if I found them. But that was a decision I could make tomorrow. First, I had to find a place to spend the night.

I asked directions to the city park. I settled on an unoccupied bench. It wasn't long before a fat teen-age boy came by and propositioned me. I let him know in no uncertain terms I wasn't interested in his advances. He went looking for other prey.

Nearby, a sailor and a girl occupied another bench. The sailor was trying to make out with the girl. She was crying and trying to say no, but the sailor kept pleading with her. Unfortunately, I fell asleep before I learned the outcome.

Pierre, S.D.

Sunday morning found me on the road again. I had chickened out on trying to locate the Websters. Instead, I hitch-hiked west towards Mitchell. I had a hankering to visit the town of Artesian, 30 miles north of Mitchell, where I spent the first six years of my life.

The temperature was a blistering 105 degrees by the time I got to Mitchell. It was unbearably hot standing on the black-top highway trying to hitch a ride. Few cars seemed to be headed towards Artesian, and none would stop to pick me up. So when I was offered a ride on west to Pierre, the capitol of South Dakota, I hopped in--anything to get out of this sun.

We arrived at Pierre--the smallest of our state capitols--about four o'clock that afternoon. To my surprise, the capitol city of the state wasn't much bigger than the county seat town of Indianola. I strolled down the main business street, went into a friendly lunch counter, and ordered a ten-cent hamburger and nickel Coke.

I began to assess my situation. It didn't look good. I was hungry. I was thirsty. I was miserable. I had no place to stay. I was down to two dollars. Things just weren't working out the way I planned. I decided to head back towards home.

The sun hung low in the sky and my heart was heavy as I trudged back out to the highway, headed back east in the direction whence I came. A car coming from the east slowed down, made a U-turn, and pulled up behind me. I thought at first it might be a policeman, but the car was too old and battered to be a police car. Besides, there was no emblem on it side.

Two men got out, one middle-aged and the other in his twenties. Both wore faded overalls. Obviously, they were farmers. The older one spoke, "Are you looking for work?"

"Yes."

"Do you know anything about farming?"

"I grew up on a farm."

"Well, we're looking for hands to help with the harvest. The pay is $20 a week plus board. Are you interested?"

It didn't take me long to make a decision. Even though farming wasn't exactly the kind of work I had in mind, it looked a lot more attractive than the alternative--which was starvation. I said I'd do it.

"Pile in," he said.

I climbed into the back seat. The younger man drove. He pulled out onto the highway and headed east, the direction whence he came.

The older man did most of the talking. He gave his name as Hiram Vaughn. Hiram was around forty-five, had weathered features, a leathery complexion, and emaciated appearance. In fact, he could readily have posed for one of those thirties-era photographic exhibits of Dust-Bowl farmers.

The younger man was Calvin Hobbes. He was almost the opposite of Hiram. Calvin was about twenty-five, unruly brown hair, muscular build, and a look of optimism. He did little talking.

I learned that Hiram and Calvin owned adjoining farms near the tiny town of Blunt, some twenty miles northeast of Pierre. Even though they farmed separately, they shared work and expenses. For example, I would be living with Hiram, but both men would contribute to my pay.

I fell asleep before we got there and could barely get my eyes open enough to stumble into the house. Exploring the place would have to wait 'til morning.

Hiram's house was a reflection of himself--weather-beaten, rundown, ramshackle. He lived alone. Every available nook and cranny was filled with oddball gadgets and implements he had accumulated over the years. They were probably worth a small fortune in antique shops. Much of the stuff had passed down from his parents and grandparents. Apparently, he never threw anything away.

We ate the noon meal at Calvin's house. His wife, Arlene, was a terrific cook. She looked the part, too, weighing in at a plump hundred and eighty pounds. She had a baby at the crawling stage who demanded lots of attention.

Hiram and Calvin were wheat farmers. Each ran a few head of range cattle, but most of their acreage was planted in grain.

I started work on Monday, July 16. My main activity was hauling wheat from the combine to the granary. It worked like this: Hiram and Calvin worked the combine together, one was on the tractor and the other on the combine. This machine cut the wheat and separated the grain from the chaff, all in one operation. As the combine moved through the field, it towed a wagon alongside which caught the separated grain as it flowed out the spout.

As soon as the wagon got full, I unhitched it, hooked another in its place, and hauled the full wagon to the granary. There, I shoveled the wheat by hand into the bins, about fifty bushels to the wagon-load. I had to hustle, as no sooner would I get one wagon empty than the next one was already full. Hiram didn't like it if they had to stop the machinery and wait for me to get back.

The harvest began to wind down around the first week in August. I gave thought to what I might do next. The idea of joining the Navy appealed to me.

I realized that without a birth certificate I couldn't merely walk into a recruiting office and ask them to induct me. There must be a way to get around that problem.

An idea hit me. I would simply register for the draft. The draft board wouldn't know the difference.

The next time Hiram drove a load of wheat to the elevator in Oneida, the county seat fifteen miles north, I asked to go along. I went into the Selective Service office and registered. No one asked me for proof of age. I told the lady I wanted to make myself available for immediate call-up. She issued me a draft registration card, thanked me for my patriotism, and told me I might expect to get my notice in a week or ten days.

The day came when the harvest was finished and my services were no longer needed on the farm. I still hadn't received my draft notice. Hiram drove me into Pierre. That's when we learned Japan had capitulated the day before. The war was over.

I slept most of Sunday in my hotel room. That evening I went to the scariest movie I had ever seen, Oscar Wilde's "Picture of Dorian Grey." The story is about an evil man who looks forever young, but his portrait reflects all his evil and immoral deeds. I couldn't bear to watch the scenes which showed the painting of the evil and ugly Dorian.

On Monday morning, I strolled down to the railroad depot to read the schedules and get some idea of where I might go next. A poster hung in the window which advertised a government job at the army ammunition storage depot at Provo, South Dakota. Transportation would be furnished, the ad said.

I looked up the address listed on the poster. The agent said the job paid $42.50 for a forty-four hour week. Applicants had to be at least eighteen years of age. I whipped out my illicitly-acquired draft card and was hired on the spot. By two that afternoon I was aboard a train headed west, ticket and meal-voucher in hand.

Provo, S.D.

Provo was a windswept town 'way down in the southwest corner of South Dakota. The area was on the fringe of the Black Hills. The town itself consisted of a few bars and businesses that catered mainly to the people who lived and worked at the Black Hills Army Ammunition Storage Depot, eleven miles further west.

The purpose of this depot was to store munitions for the U.S. Army. It was sprawled over hundreds and hundreds of acres of land with bunkers and storage sheds. These were spaced far enough apart so if one blew up--either by accident or enemy action--none of the others would be endangered. It was a regular army base run by the military, but most of the people who worked there were civilians.

As far as I was concerned, it was almost like being in the Army. The workers lived on the base. Married people had their own quarters. Single people lived in barracks, two to a room. On certain nights we were allowed to go into town; otherwise, we played sports or hung around the civilian PX.

I worked with a crew that handled artillery shells ranging in size from 75 mm to 155 mm. The 75's weighed 35 pounds and were fairly easy to lug around. The 155's weighed in at 98 pounds. A full day of manhandling these brutes provided more exercise than I really wanted.

Apparently, most of the munitions we received for storage were shipped back from the European war theater. A lot of the shells had handwritten hate messages on them, or drawings of Hitler and Mussolini.

A remote section of the base contained a closely-guarded area where chemical weapons were destroyed. I visited that area only once.

After six weeks, I no longer found the work interesting or challenging. I developed an urge to move on.

Sheridan, Wyoming

Sheridan, Wyoming, was my next destination. I had learned about it from one of the young soldiers on the base. It was his home town. He talked about it so enthusiastically that I couldn't wait to get there. I handed in my resignation, collected my final paycheck, and bought a train ticket to Sheridan.

Sheridan was a town time had passed by. The streets, stores, and people looked exactly as I imagined they looked in the eighteen-hundreds. Hardly a thing had changed since General Custer passed by here on his way to the Little Big Horn. With a population of 20,000, this frontier town was nestled at the foot of the Big Horn Mountains, scarcely more than a stone's throw from the Montana border.

I found work with Peter Kewitt Construction Company, an international firm that built bridges and dams all over the world. They had a contract to build a bridge across the south fork of the Tongue River in the mountains sixty miles above Sheridan.

The site was known as Bondi's Lodge. As one might suspect, it was a hunting lodge named for its owner, Mr. Bondi. I bunked with other members of the construction gang in a large, log bunkhouse. Our sole source of heat was a king-sized fireplace. We took our meals at the lodge. Sometimes we'd gather there in the evening to drink beer and swap stories.

On Saturday nights we all piled in pickups and drove down to Sheridan, returning again on Sunday nights. During my stays in Sheridan, I usually hung around places like the saddle-maker's shop or the gunsmith's, fascinated to watch a different way of life.

My job classification was loosely referred to as a "grunt." That's an unskilled laborer who does whatever tasks are assigned. Some days I worked on the scaffolding high above the water, other days I might work in the cofferdams, well below the water level, mucking out seepage.

Hauling cement was the hardest work. Another grunt and I would drive down to Ranchester, a town halfway down the mountain. Each bag of cement weighed 72 pounds. We hand-carried them from a rail car and loaded them on a flat-bed trailer. It took more than 200 bags to make a full load. We were pooped at the end of the day.

Winter set in. High in the mountains, the cold weather comes on fast. I didn't have any cold-weather clothes and it got pretty uncomfortable working out of doors, particularly when it was windy. That led me to start thinking about moving on.

My closest friend on the construction gang was another grunt named Ray Walker. Ray was eighteen, wore seaman's garb, and claimed to have served in the Merchant Marines. He was short, muscular, and looked the part of a sailor. The two of us talked a lot about finding a warmer climate.

Ray and I pored over highway maps obtained from a gas station and decided on San Angelo, Texas. Neither of us had any contacts there, it just seemed like a nice place to spend the winter. If we had known more about Texas, however, we probably would have chosen San Antonio or the Rio Grande Valley. Our mode of travel would be the only means we knew, which was to ride "old lady thumb."

We collected our final paychecks in Sheridan, and on Monday thumbed our way southward. Rides were hard to come by. We made it only as far as Casper by nightfall. That was not good. We had planned to conserve our meager money supply by sleeping in the great out of doors. We gave it a try: we wrapped ourselves in our coats and stretched out in the ditch beside the highway intersection. However, the temperature got so cold that all we could do was shiver and shake. Sometime after midnight we gave up. We hiked two miles into town and spent the rest of the night sleeping on chairs in an unlocked hotel lobby. The clerk was decidedly unhappy next morning when she saw us flaked out there.

We walked the two miles back to the highway. There was a fair amount of southbound traffic but no one willing to give us a ride. We got discouraged. We began wondering if perhaps people might be afraid to have two scruffy-looking strangers in the car with them. Who knows, we might be carrying a knife or a gun.

We agreed to split up and travel separately. We said we'd meet again at the Union Bus Station in Denver.

Denver

I waited in vain for two days at the Denver bus station. No Ray. I figured he must have turned tail and returned to Sheridan.

Union Bus Station was a busy place in November, 1945. Thousands of servicemen and civilian travelers shuttled through daily.

That made it ideal as a hangout for runaways and vagrants. I fit right in. No one questioned what I was doing there. The station had an "annex" waiting room across the alley which had less foot traffic. That's where I slept.

I got acquainted with two runaway girls who hung around the station, Thelma Shaw and Bobbie Reynolds. Thelma was medium height, sturdy build, with mousy brown hair. She had brown-stained teeth she said was caused by the natural fluoridation in the water at Colorado Springs where she was from. Bobbie was the taller of the two, more slender, dark-haired, prettier, and somewhat aloof. She didn't talk much. Bobbie took up with me, perhaps as her protector against some of the more unsavory characters hanging around.

After three nights in the bus station, I said good-bye to the girls and bought a ticket to the nearest town south of Denver. From there I started hitch-hiking again. I was still bent on getting to San Angelo. I made it as far as Raton, New Mexico, that night.

Raton, N.M.

Raton was a sleepy little town of eight thousand souls. Its economic activity was divided between railroading and ranching.

The town was located at the southern terminus of the Raton Pass, the only major north-south passage through the southern Colorado mountains for a hundred miles in either direction. It was also the place where the trains changed crews. The population was about half Mexican and half Anglo.

I took a room at the "Love Hotel." It was a walk-up, second-floor establishment above a dry-goods store that advertised low-cost accommodations. The price was a dollar a night or five dollars for the week. The owner-manager was a middle-aged couple, Sidney and Margaret Love. Sidney had been crippled by polio as a child. His legs were encased in iron braces, but he got around nimbly with the aid of crutches.

For some unknown reason, Raton appealed to me. I decided to stick around for a few days.

The best place to pick up day work, I discovered, was at the pool hall a half block up the street. People used it as a kind of hiring hall.

I worked three days cleaning up a rental house owned by the man who ran the watch repair shop next door. That paid fifty cents an hour. Then I worked four days at the fair barn cleaning stalls after the close of a big cattle show. For two days I pushed a wheelbarrow on a construction site pouring a foundation for a new house. That paid seventy-five cents an hour.

My most interesting job was also the most dangerous: bucking slabs at a sawmill. I hired on at a small, independent sawmill a few miles west of town. It was run by the owner and his son. They lived in town and picked me up every morning for the drive to work.

The "slabs" were the rough, outer, unusable parts of the log that were cut off during the log's first pass through the mill. On a large log, a single slab might weigh 200 pounds. I worked close to a spinning saw blade six feet in diameter and had no guard or shield.

The routine called for me to catch the slabs as they came off the blade. One slip and I would be hamburger. I tossed slabs onto a tram-cart that ran on a pair of rails. When the cart became full, I pushed it out to the end of the track, tilted it up, and dumped the load onto a pile of scrap on the hillside below.

My job came to an abrupt end when I overloaded the tram one

day. In pushing the overloaded cart out to the end of the track, I lost control and it flipped over and tossed me twenty feet down to the ground. The fall badly injured my left knee.

No longer able to do strenuous work until my leg healed, I found work as a dishwasher at the Park Avenue Cafe. It was located on Park Avenue one block east of Main. The restaurant was a popular eatery for off-duty railroad crews.

Hugh Bunch was the owner and operator. He was a large, jovial, gregarious fellow who had driven Greyhound buses for many years until he developed palsy and had to come in from the road. Hugh was in his early forties. His wife, Priscilla, was several years younger.

One day I happened to glance out the serving window into the restaurant. Sitting there in one of the booths was Thelma Shaw, one of the girls I met in Denver. She was by herself and looked rather forlorn. I took off my apron and went out to talk with her. She remembered me.

Thelma said the police had run her out of Denver. She had gotten a ride this far, but now she was broke, hungry, and desperate for a place to stay.

I sprang for the price of a meal and told her I thought I could get her a room at the Love Hotel. I phoned Sidney Love and told him I'd pay for her room.

That night, Thelma came to my room to express her gratitude. She said Sidney offered her a job as a maid and she would be living at the hotel. She spent the night, the night after that, and a whole series of nights. Two lost souls had found each other.

The next month was one of the happiest I can remember. Thelma and I saw each other constantly.

But it was too good to last. One night shortly after Christmas, I came back to the hotel after work and found Thelma gone. I knocked on the manager's door. Sidney Love told me the sheriff's deputies had taken her away. She was being returned to her family in Colorado Springs.

The area surrounding Raton suddenly became attractive for oil and gas exploration and drilling. Several rigs moved into the area. Many of the crew members ate at the Park Avenue Cafe, particularly on weekends. Vic Hupfield, one of the rig workers whom I knew, asked one evening, "How would you like to roughneck?"

Not being familiar with oil rig terminology, I thought the guy wanted to wrestle. I replied hesitantly, "That wouldn't be fair, would it? You're a lot bigger than I am."

Vic and his buddies laughed uproariously. They explained that "roughnecking" was a term used to describe work on a well-drilling rig. It's not the same as "roughhousing."

The next three weeks I roughnecked on a rig near Clayton, New Mexico. Clayton was about seventy-five miles east, near the Texas-Oklahoma border. This was the town where famed outlaw Billy the Kid was shot by Sheriff Pat Garrison. On our way to the well site, we passed Mount Capulan, said to be one of the most perfect volcano cones in the world. A spiral road wound its way to the top.

The well came in dry. So had several other wells in the area--either dry or marginally producing. This convinced the drilling company to pull up stakes and move to another part of the country. Once again, I was out of a job.

Homeward Bound

I found myself thinking about home. I'd shown that I could make my own way in the world. There was nothing more for me to prove, either to myself or others. In my own eyes, I was no longer a boy. I was a man. This enabled me to return to Iowa on my own terms.

I said my good-byes to Sidney Love, Hugh Bunch, and a few other people I knew, walked down to the highway going east, and stuck out my thumb.

I got lucky. An industrial products salesman on his way to Amarillo, Texas, picked me up. It didn't take brains to figure out why he wanted company on the ride. That trip across the Texas panhandle was the longest stretch of unbroken highway I had ever seen.

I spent the night at the Union Bus Station. A fat, funny-looking little man came around and tried to pick me up by offering a nice warm bed to sleep in. I declined the offer. The guy didn't seem discouraged. He moved on down the line to proposition the next guy, and the next. As near as I could tell, he didn't have any luck.

Heading out of Amarillo the next day, I followed Route 66 into Oklahoma. Instead of going through Oklahoma City, however, I decided to cut north on highway 81 to Enid and on to Wichita and Kansas City.

A major snowstorm was moving in by the time I got to Enid. I took refuge in the bus terminal. That worked out fine until midnight when the terminal closed. I found myself out on the street in the midst of a blizzard.

A short distance down the street was a taxicab company that was open all night. I made up some cock-and-bull story about having missed my bus, and the dispatcher let me in. I spent the rest of the night bullshitting with the various drivers as they came and went.

Several inches of snow had accumulated by morning. I trudged back over to the bus station to wait for the weather to improve enough for me to hit the road. Having gotten little sleep the night before, my eyelids grew heavy, and I soon fell fast asleep. The next thing I knew, a policeman was tapping me on the bottom of my foot with his nightstick. The cop asked me some questions--who was I, what was I doing here, and where was I going. Apparently dissatisfied with the answers I gave, he hauled me off to jail.

For the next two days I languished in the Enid jail. In some respects, that was a pleasant interlude. I was out of the storm. My quarters were clean, warm and comfortable. The food was good. And I got caught up on my sleep.

A deputy came to my cell on Friday morning and told me to get my gear together. They had run a background check on me and didn't find any record or warrants, so they were setting me free. He and another deputy drove me to the edge of town, put me out of the car, and told me not to be seen around there anymore.

I was happy to oblige.

It was slow going until I got past Wichita. On the outskirts of town I caught a truck driver who carried me all the way to Kansas City.

By midnight I was at Cameron, Missouri, where I'd spent the night eight months before. I went behind the same signboard and tried to get some sleep. Near-freezing February temperatures made sleep impossible. Moreover, the truck-stop restaurant across the street was closed, so there was little I could do but huddle against the cold.

Daybreak found me back on the road with my thumb hanging out. I caught a couple of good rides and was in Indianola by ten in the morning.

I went to Uncle Harry's house. Only Hazel and Flora were home. They said Dad no longer lived there, that he had moved to the southeastern part of town.

Flora said, "Happy Birthday, James."

Until then, I hadn't realized that today was my sixteenth birthday, February 16, 1946.

They say, when you gain a lover
You begin to lose a friend,
That the end of the beginning
Is the beginning of the end.
They say the moment that you're born
Is when you start to die,
And the first time that we said Hello
Began our last goodbye.
--"First Hello, Last Goodbye"
--Roger Whittaker

13

The End of the Beginning

Dad took my return in stride and didn't show a great deal of emotion. It was as if his son had been gone a mere seven days rather than seven months. He didn't inquire as to where I'd been, what I'd done, or why I came back. On the other hand, Dad didn't curse me out either--which was a relief.

During my absence, Dad had started a small, independent construction business. He acquired an old 1928 Chevrolet three-quarter ton, stake-bed truck that he got for $125. His sole employee was Vergil Scoggins, a scrawny, hair-lipped, timid soul who lived east of town with a painfully shy wife and two ragamuffin children. A born loser if there ever was one.

Dad asked me what I planned to do. "Get a job, I guess," I replied.

"Well, I've got a contract to put a new foundation under a house over on East Ashland Street. We can use an extra hand. You can work on that...if you want a job."

That contract typified the kinds of jobs Dad got--too big for a handyman, not big enough for a full-service contractor.

This was an old house. The timbers had rotted out underneath and the foundation was sagging. Dad raised it up on jacks, tore out the old foundation, poured new concrete footings, laid a concrete-block foundation, replaced the cross-beams under the floor joists, and sat it back on its new foundation.

Dad's handling of the finances on this job also typified his dealings. He agreed to a fixed-price sum for doing the work. The job turned out to be bigger than he estimated and he barely broke even on the deal.

Eugene Alexander was just not a good businessman. He'd quote a job off the top of his head, never working up a bid sheet. Invariably the job would take longer and cost more than his "guesstimate." Consequently, he never got ahead in business.

Types of jobs he successfully bid on ranged from digging up and replacing a collapsed sewer pipe, to digging a basement and building the foundation for a house to be moved onto, replacing old roofs, rehabilitating old houses, repairing and rebuilding garages, and replacing defective brick chimneys.

I discovered a hidden talent, namely, a knack for plastering. Soon I was getting most of the plastering jobs that came our way. That sparked an interesting reversal of roles between Dad and me. The "boss" mixed the plaster and carried the hod to his sixteen-year-old son who performed the role of skilled craftsman.

I got most of the chimney jobs too. A lot of old houses in the area had chimneys whose mortar was disintegrating and falling away. This, in turn, created a fire hazard. The job involved tearing the chimney down to the roof line and rebuilding it with new bricks and mortar. Dad was quite comfortable with me scrambling around on slanted roofs. He stayed down on the ground and assisted me, the skilled worker, by passing bricks and mortar up to the roof-top.

My personal relations with Dad were markedly different from those before I left. I lived at home, paid rent, and worked for Dad. But the old domineering pattern no longer existed. I was cast more in the role of an adult son, emotionally independent, free to go and come as I pleased without interference. Dad accepted it that way.

Not that we didn't have arguments from time to time. But these tended to take place more on an adult-adult level rather than a parent-child model. Not once did Dad try to assert his once-domineering authority over me.

An ongoing problem I had with Dad concerned the fact he didn't keep books. He ran the business on a cash-only basis. As a result, Dad often fell behind in meeting payroll obligations, including mine. Sometimes the back-pay owed me built up to fairly sizable amounts. Whenever I tried to collect, Dad either had a faulty memory or offered some feeble excuse why he couldn't pay me right then.

Early in the summer a house became available with even cheaper rent--$5 per month. It fronted on east-west Highway 92 and was nearly back-to-back with Dad's present domicile. Also, it sat on a bigger lot.

The cheap rent was due to the county health department which had condemned it. Among other health hazards cited, it had standing water in the basement. Dad planned to live in it only until the owner tore it down.

Having a larger lot meant that Dad could accumulate more animals. Before long he had fourteen goats, five 4-H club calves, and three or four stray dogs--all on a city lot. Dad was in perpetual trouble with his neighbors because the calves kept getting out and destroying their gardens.

Dad's rattle-trap truck became both a source of amusement among townsfolk and a source of embarrassment for his kids. In an effort to dress it up, he gave it a new coat of paint. He applied the paint by brush, which left a matte finish and lots of uneven spots where the original color showed through. The shade was robin's egg blue.

That blue truck became a regular sight clatter-banging around town. Some hangers-on at the gas station derisively dubbed it the "Bluebird Special."

I did my part to give the truck a more professional appearance. I applied a hand-lettered sign on each side that read:

Alexander Construction Company
Indianola, Iowa

The 1928 model Chevy truck wasn't equipped with a starter. It had to be cranked by hand.

One frosty morning, the engine was balky. I spun the crank in an effort to get it to start. The dang thing backfired, causing the crank handle to spin backwards viciously and hit me on the back of my hand. It cracked a bone in my wrist. So for the next several weeks I sported a neat little cast on my right hand.

Since that truck was the family's only means of transportation, Dad took it to Des Moines to attend the 1946 State Fair, Iowa's centennial year. The kids rode in back. (I was not along.)

Catherine was so embarrassed she hunkered down under a blanket so none of her friends would see her. She poked her head out occasionally to see where they were.

The main north-south highway through Indianola was U.S. 65. It was also a heavily-traveled truck route. Many of the truckers stopped of at the Sale Barn Cafe on the south edge of town.

Long-haul drivers, most of whom were in their twenties, seemed to me and my friends like "kings of the road." Most were based out of Missouri, and their trucks sported intriguing names like Sedalia, Carthage, Springfield and Joplin. I made friends with several of these drivers and visualized myself becoming one of them some day.

One noon in early July, Floyd Manders and I were sitting around the Sale Barn Cafe and idly speculating as to why so many of these trucks originated in Missouri. Floyd, like me, was a high school dropout. Tall, skinny, and with a hook-nose, he looked a lot like Huntz Hall of Dead End Kids fame.

We decided maybe we should take a look-see for ourselves. So with no more forethought than that, and without telling anybody we were leaving, we sauntered out to the edge of the highway, stuck out our thumbs, and hitched a ride south. Since we planned only to be gone a couple of days, we didn't carry anything with us, not even a toothbrush.

We were passing through Chillicothe, Missouri, sixty miles south of the border, when the police picked us up and hauled us off to jail. They asked a few questions, then put us in a holding cell while they checked our stories.

At about nine-thirty that evening, an Iowa state trooper came up to Dad's door and bluntly stated, "Your boy's run away again. Do you want to pay to have him brought back this time?"

Dad told the trooper, "No. I'm not paying to bring him back. I don't care what you do with him."

Early next morning, the police turned me loose and told me I was free to do what I wanted. As for Floyd, they said he would have to stay because his dad was driving down to pick him up.

I hitched a ride north and arrived home by noon. My little escapade lasted barely twenty-four hours. Yet it created quite a stir. People were saying, "Have you heard? James ran away again."

Of course, I never intended to run away. Floyd and I were just making a little side trip. It never occurred to me that anybody would be upset by my being gone a couple of days.

The Alexanders were moving up in the world. Or so it seemed. Dad acquired three residential lots in the eleven-hundred block of West Detroit Street. The property lay at the western city limits. Detroit Street dead-ended just past our property line at a small farm owned by the Burrell family.

Dad had visions of building a house on one lot and holding the other two for speculation. The property sloped sharply downward from the street. Dad's plan was to build a walk-in basement into the side of the hill.

The construction sequence was to build the basement level first, move into that, then build the upper level sometime in the future as money became available. He borrowed $800 from Roxie's mother to start construction.

A more pressing problem came up. The owner of the house we now lived in had exhausted all his appeals. The building was soon to be torn down. Where would we live in the interim?

Dad's solution was to build temporary living quarters on the back side of the property, a building that could later be used as a small barn or storage shed. Vergil and I pitched in, and within three weeks had thrown up a shed twelve-by-twenty feet, one-and-a-half stories high, and unpainted.

For economic reasons, Dad used green, uncured lumber. Green lumber was cheap. Dad reasoned that since he didn't plan on living in it very long he wouldn't have to worry about the wood warping and cracking.

Living in that shed was a lot like camping out. Catherine and Shirley slept upstairs in the loft with just a few blankets as mattresses. Downstairs was a single room that encompassed a kitchen, table and chairs, and Dad and Roxie's bed.

Dick and I slept in a borrowed tent we pitched a few yards away.

I dug a trench and constructed a one-hole outdoor privy.

Dad was finally able to re-introduce cattle into his life. This time through two of his children. More particularly, he wanted Dick to become a "cattle man" like he had been. Dick seemed a willing participant.

He built a cattle pen on the back side of the shed. It bordered against the back wall where the cattle could look in the window and watch the people inside. The girls found it a weird feeling to look out the window and see a steer peering in at them.

Dad took Dick down to the Sale Barn and bought a couple of calves. They had to be a certain kind, special calves that had potential for 4-H showing. This 4-H project let Dad and Dick spend many happy hours together. Dad passed on his considerable knowledge about feeding, grooming, and showing calves.

Shirley was drawn in on the act, too. Dad bought her a calf to care for and train for the show ring--although Dick ended up doing most of the actual work. Dad thought there would be a special advantage for a ten-year-old girl to be in the ring with a large calf.

When it came time for the Warren County Fair, they loaded the calves into a trailer and hauled them out to the fairgrounds. Dad made Dick spend the night in the stall with the calves. Shirley got to sleep at home.

The day of the judging, Dick's calf won a blue ribbon. In contrast, Shirley's calf was disqualified because it did not have the appropriate vaccinations. Dad argued and argued with the judges, but to no avail.

Later, Shirley watched her calf being sold at auction and led off to the slaughter house. She decided right then and there she was not cut out for that kind of activity.

Dick was an outdoor, rough-and-tumble guy through and through. He loved roughhousing, fishing, hunting, and walking the creeks with his buddies.

He took up boxing. Almost daily he'd stage boxing matches with his friends out back or, depending on the weather, inside the tent.

One day Shirley was playing nearby and Dick got the idea it would be fun to see a girl fight with boxing gloves. He called her over and tried to get her to put on the gloves for a bout with the younger brother of one of his friends.

Shirley protested, "No, no."

The boys teased her and called her a baby until she finally relented. With much trepidation she put on the boxing gloves.

The two ten-year-olds--boy against girl--were taken to the center of the make-shift ring and told to go at it. Shirley was so scared she closed her eyes and swung her arm with the biggest round-house swing she could manage. She connected with something, opened her eyes to see what she had hit, and saw her opponent lying flat on the ground.

The boys were shocked. Shirley quietly took off the boxing

gloves and walked out of the ring. Dick never again asked her to box with the boys.

Work progressed on the house slowly throughout the summer. It wasn't until cold weather arrived that Dad got motivated. Then he worked every night and weekend trying to beat the snow. The work involved excavating the ground, pouring a concrete slab floor, laying concrete block outer walls, raising the interior walls, and laying planks for the flat roof. The roof was ultimately intended to be the floor of the second story when the house was finished.

Thanksgiving came. Snow was on the ground and we hadn't moved into the basement house yet. As usual, Dad had mismanaged his money and didn't have enough to finish.

The shed was no place to spend the winter. It had no interior paneling or insulation. The green lumber siding had so many cracks and spaces that the wind just whistled through. In fact, one could see through the cracks from the outside.

Roxie tried to roast a chicken that I brought home for Thanksgiving dinner. Even the stove wouldn't heat enough for the chicken to get done. Dick and I continued to sleep in the tent.

I took matters into my own hands. One thawing December day, I walked down to the lumber yard, explained our dire situation to the owner, and talked him into extending credit for enough roofing paper, nails and sealant to waterproof the roof. Not only that, I talked him into delivering it for me.

The lumber yard owner later commented the only reason he did it was because he was impressed with my pluck and courage.

By the time Dad got home that evening, I had the job done. He was totally surprised. He was even more shocked to learn I had completed the entire job by myself except for a little help the last hour or so from Dick when he got home from school.

To be sure, the job wasn't perfect. The first snow-melt revealed a few leaks that had to have a little more tar smeared on them. But at least the family had a warm and reasonably dry place to move into.

When we moved in, there was no electricity in the house. Dad couldn't afford the hook-up costs. So once again, I took charge. On my own initiative, I ran electrical wiring out to the utility pole and hooked onto a transformer. Inside, I wired overhead lights in each room. I made no attempt to wire the wall outlets. I figured that for the time being, it would be sufficient to run a patchwork of extension cords and plug in whatever appliances we needed.

Eventually, Dad found an ex-navy electrician attending Simpson College on the GI Bill who did a little "moonlighting" at non-union wages. He came out a couple of evenings to wire the house properly. He said he was amazed that a sixteen-year-old dropout, without ever having studied electricity, had done everything right.

If ever someone were to invent a magnet to attract junky things, he should name it after Eugene Alexander. It didn't take long for our property to look like a city dump. Dad dragged home anything that other people wanted to throw away--old baby strollers, high chairs, broken-down beds. It was always his plan to fix and paint them for resale. It never happened.

Catherine was so embarrassed by Dad's mess that she wouldn't tell people this was where she lived; instead she'd point to the White's house across the street. If offered a ride home from school or the skating rink, she'd have the person drop her off at Mrs. White's house. She'd walk slowly up onto the porch and wait for the driver to get out of sight, and only then, when the coast was clear, would she walk across the street to her own home.

Catherine's home-ec class took on a special project for Christmas. The students voted to plan a Christmas party for underprivileged children. They baked cookies, planned refreshments, put up decorations and organized games. All in all, it was a grand affair.

Catherine was absolutely mortified to discover her own family's name on the list.

Shirley went to the party wearing her only good dress--a sailor dress that Catherine had bought her. Her best shoes were run over at the heels and had holes in the soles. Nevertheless, Shirley was such a happy little thing at the party she probably never knew how embarrassed Catherine was.

Now almost sixteen and a high school sophomore, Catherine had her first boyfriend. His name was Jerome Brunner and he was from Milo, twelve miles southeast of Indianola. Being the typical big brother, I teased her unmercifully. One evening I answered the door when Jerome came to the house to pick her up. He introduced himself in a gentlemanly manner. "I'm Jerome Brunner, and I've come to take Catherine to the dance."

I called out in a loud voice, "Catherine, your *Romeo* is here!"

She hissed, "James, shut up!" It was several days before she would speak to me again.

Catherine quit her job at the Sale Barn Cafe in mid-winter because the weather got too cold for her to walk all the way across town. For a while, she cleaned houses for fifty cents an hour. It gave her a strange feeling to clean a house on Saturday, then go to school with those same people on Monday.

She applied for a job at The Diner cafe, which was an old railroad car turned into a lunch counter. It afforded a much shorter walk than the Sale Barn. The owner offered her the job but wanted her to quit school and work full time. She told them, "No, it doesn't make sense to quit school for just a piddlin' waitress job."

I buddied around with a group of guys who had returned from military service. These included my cousin Roscoe, back from the Navy; Bob Heaviland, army POW; Bill Wheeler, who fought through Italy; Don Sandy, ex-marine; and Roger LaPlante, paratrooper in the 81st Airborne. These ex-GI's formed what was loosely referred to as the "Fifty-two Twenty Club." The reference, of course, was to the severance benefit of $20 a week for fifty-two weeks which ex-GI's were entitled to while seeking civilian employment. I felt more comfortable hanging around with guys than with boys my own age. Probably, my seven months on the road had matured me to the poiint where I no longer had much in common with fellow sixteen-year-olds.

There was never any doubt in my mind but that I would join the Navy as soon as I turned seventeen. The week before my seventeenth birthday I hitch-hiked to Des Moines and told the Navy recruiting officer I wanted to sign up. He was happy to oblige.

I filled out the usual paperwork that asked a lot of questions about my history and background, including record of arrests. The chief said they'd have to check my eligibility. I was afraid my two arrests, one in Belton, Missouri, and the other in Enid, Oklahoma, might work against me. The chief called me a few days later to say my eligibility checked out OK. and that I needed to come back for a physical and some placement testing.

Without a high school education, my highest hope was to qualify for Machinist Mate so I could learn to repair engines, or even better, Aviation Machinist Mate to learn to work on airplane engines. My test scores came back. I had scored in the top five percent. The chief said I was qualified for Electronics Technician school.

"What's 'electronics?'" I asked.

'I don't really know either," the chief replied. "But it's the navy's top program. Electronics Technician is a brand new rating. I think you'd better take it." I said yes.

March 3, 1947, dawned cold and blustery. The winter's snow had melted except for a few dirty patches. During daytime, the sun thawed the wet ground and turned it into gooey mud, and at night the ground froze again and turned the mud into bone-jarring ruts. The barren trees had not yet put forth their buds. It was Iowa at its ugliest.

At ten o'clock that night I shook the mud of Iowa from my feet and boarded the train to San Diego...and a new life. No one came to the station to see me off.

That summer, Dad pulled up stakes and moved the family to a farm near Morris, Illinois. He had found a job doing what he knew best, working around cattle.

Of his five kids, Dad had only Dick and Shirley left at home. Catherine stayed behind in Indianola to finish high school, David was living with Harry, and I escaped to the Navy.

Author's Concluding Personal Postscript

The Roman god Janus is the god of the new year. As such, he serves as symbol of endings and beginnings. Janus has two faces back to back. One face looks back upon the past, the other face looks forward towards the future not yet written.

In a similar fashion, the year 1947 was a time of endings and beginnings for the Alexander kids. That year brought an end to one era in our saga. At the same time it ushered in a period of new beginnings: me in the U.S. Navy, Catherine supporting herself through school, and Dad starting his second family on new soil.

We were better off by 1947, but none of us who had ever lived through those Depression years could ever forget them.

We survived through faith, hope and charity, and by hanging on to each other.

It was a time of great anxiety and human suffering. But all of us were, in one fashion or another, strengthened by those difficult and perilous times.

Dad, for all his shortcomings, did the best job he knew how to raise us. Despite our feelings of abandonment, abusiveness, and degrading poverty, all five of us kids turned out pretty good.

We had survived.

§ § §

14

Epilogue

The inspiring story is how the children overcame their backgrounds and became successful in life. The narrative ended in 1947, but the record doesn't end there. Accordingly, here are their accounts, beginning with the parents:

James Eugene Alexander

Eugene returned to his first love, working with show cattle. He was employed by various breeders until 1957 when ill health caused him to move to California, where he worked in a plastics factory. Four children were born to his second family. Eugene died in Arlington, Texas, in March 1985, a few days shy of his seventy-fifth birthday. He is buried next to his parents at Rising Sun Cemetery, Altoona, Iowa.

Lillian Gamble Alexander Evans

Lillian migrated to Las Vegas, Nevada, where she worked as a waitress and hostess at several major resort hotels. She remarried in 1953. Lillian retired in 1973 and moved to Brighton, Colorado, to be near Dick's widow, Juanita, and her five fatherless children. In 1980, she moved to a retirement center in Garden Grove, California, near her daughter Catherine. She died in June 1985 and lies buried in Palm Cemetery, Las Vegas, next to her mother and second husband.

James Edwin Alexander

James is former Dean of the Meinders School of Business at Oklahoma City University. He served eight years active duty in the U.S. Navy from 1947 to 1955, attained the rank of Chief Warrant Officer, and received combat decorations during the Korean War. He attended the University of the Pacific (B.A.,

1959), Boston University (S.T.B., M.Th., 1962), Claremont Graduate School (M.A., Ph.D. Cand. 1969), and Vanderbilt University (Ph.D., 1972), with additional studies at Harvard, The Wharton School, and Vanderbilt School of Law. He is an ordained Methodist minister, has taught at several universities, and served as a senior executive of the United Methodist Church. He is the author of twenty books and is listed in *Who's Who of the World,* and *Who's Who in Finance and Industry.* He resides in Oklahoma City, OK, with his wife and fellow author, Ann Lacy.

Catherine Aline Alexander Cargill

Catherine moved to California in 1948 when she graduated from high school. She later went to work for Trans World Airlines, retiring in 1993 with 25 years of service. She lives in Southern California near her two sons and four grandchildren.

Her travels have carried her to virtually every corner of the globe, including such exotic places as Argentina, Australia, Egypt, Greece, Italy, Morocco, New Zealand, Portugal, Spain, and more than a dozen other countries. For a poor little country girl who once couldn't afford a toothbrush, Catherine has traveled farther in life than she ever dared to dream.

Richard Eugene Alexander

Dick enlisted in the U.S. Navy in 1950. After four years of service, he settled in Las Vegas, NV, where he met and married Juanita Lozano. Dick returned to military service in the U.S. Army. He served in the Army Security Agency for fourteen years, primarily in radio communications. Tours of duty included Ethiopia, Washington, Japan, Panama, and two tours in Viet Nam.

Dick served his country proudly and was a loving father and husband. He was athletic, and he passed on his love for sports to his five children by training and coaching them in baseball, football, and scouting.

Dick died in the service of his country during the Viet Nam War, February 28, 1971. He was buried with military honors at the National Cemetery, Fort Logan, Colorado.

Shirley Ann Alexander Patterson

Shirley moved to Des Moines in the summer of 1953 to work at Hotel Fort Des Moines and subsequently at Traveler's Insurance Company. She married Estel "Pete" Patterson and they moved to Texas. Shirley graduated from the University of Texas, Arlington (B.S.) and North Texas State University (M.L.S). Currently, she and Pete reside in Texas near their three children and eight grandchildren.

David Dean Alexander

David graduated from Indianola High School in 1958 as a football and track star. He entered college on a football scholarship; however, he was dropped from the scholarship roll when he suffered an injury. He enlisted in the U.S. Army, and served as a cadet tactics instructor at the U.S. Military Academy, West Point. He graduated from the University of Northern Colorado at Greely (B.S., M.S., and E.D.S.), and currently works as a psychologist at the Missouri State Correctional Facility.

David was a noted pipe carver for several years. He was commissioned to carve likenesses of President Ronald Reagan and England's Prince Charles for the 1982 World's Fair.

9 780939 965199